CURATED TRUE CRIME

RITUAL KILLERS

MURDER, MADNESS AND MAYHEM
BOOK 1

JAMIE MALTON

AIDEN GALWAY

MP

Malton
Publishing
LLC

WORD OF WARNING

THE DETAILS WRITTEN in these stories come directly from eyewitness accounts, interviews, court transcripts, crime scenes, and autopsy reports. Due to the graphic nature of the crimes featured in *Curated True Crime* which include: murder, domestic violence, sexual assault, hate crimes, sex work, incest, mental illness, child abuse, animal abuse, abduction, suicide, mutilation, and necrophilia, reader discretion is advised.

GET A FREE BOOK, AND MORE

1. As a thank you to my readers, I created a special volume of my other series *Killer Case Files: 20 All New True Crime Stories.* You can download it right now in e-book or audiobook for FREE at this link. https://dl.book funnel.com/tf4q1gethc or go to JamieMalton.com for more information/

2. Would you like to join my **Launch Team** and receive a free volume before it's published?

If you are a reviewer on any of the well-known platforms like Amazon, Goodreads, or Instagram, you could receive an advance review copy of my future volumes. I'd love to have you on my official launch team!

Please go to JamieMalton.com and sign up on my mailing list for more information.

Thank you for being a reader.

Sincerely,

Jamie Malton

DEMON DEAL

Nineteen-year-old Danyal Hussein made a deal with a demon and signed his contract in blood. He'd spent years researching how to do it by watching videos created by a man named Matthew Lawrence. Incarcerated in Utah, Lawrence was part of the *Satanist Order of Nine Angles*, an occultist group. Danyal also actively participated in a Satanic forum overseen by Lawrence and adhered to Lawrence's guidance on how to form an agreement with a demon. Danyal decided he was willing to make the necessary sacrifices to get what he wanted.

Below is the agreement Danyal wrote with pencil and paper.

London 2020

Agreement
For the mighty King Lucifuge Rofocale

- Perform a minimum of six sacrifices every six months for as long as I am free and physically capable.

   -Sacrifice only women

   -Build a temple for you

   -Do everything that I have promised

For me

   -win the Mega Millions Super Jackpot

- ~~Recieve~~- To Receive fruitful rewards in return for the future sacrifices I make to you, the rewards could consist of wealth and power.

   -To never be suspected of any crimes by the police, and also that the police will never know of any crimes that I have done and that I will do.

   Signed by:

Me: Danyal

       King Lucifuge Rofocale:

The British government knew about Danyal's growing obsession with far-right extremism, satanism, and occult practices, and they tried to intervene. He was enrolled in *Prevent*, a government program to counter religious extremism. Danyal was placed in the part of the program designed to address the most severe and at-risk cases. Regular meetings were scheduled to monitor Danyal's progress and ensure his path did not veer toward a dangerous outcome. Danyal completed the programs, but in the end, it did little to deter him.

～

Two remarkable sisters, Nicole Smallman a freelance photographer, and Bibaa Henry, a social worker, had an unbreakable bond. Nicole, aged 27, and Bibaa, aged 46, were adored by their friends and family.

On the evening of June 5th, Bibaa's birthday, the sisters gathered with friends at Fryent Country Park. The park was decorated with fairy lights, and the evening started as a lovely experience for everyone who attended. As the night wore on, their party-goers departed, leaving the sisters to finish their celebration alone; however, this birthday celebration would soon become a nightmare.

The sisters never returned home. The next day, their family searched desperately, hoping to find them unharmed. The search lasted three days, and unfortunately, Bibaa's partner, Adam, was the one who made the horrifying discovery. He was searching in the park and was on the phone with the police when he stumbled upon the bodies of the two sisters lying intertwined in a dark hedge.

The Metropolitan Police investigation started immediately. The autopsy found that Bibaa had been stabbed eight times, and Nicole had been stabbed 28 times. The police discovered blood at the crime scene that didn't belong to the sisters. Their murderer had injured himself in the attack. A DNA profile from the blood led police to a partial match of someone already in their system, Kamal Hussein, the father of Danyal Hussein. Kamal's DNA had been registered with the police during a different investigation on something unrelated. Police searched the Hussein residence and uncovered a chilling scene. Danyal's bedroom was a portal to a world of darkness, with satanic paraphernalia strewn about and multiple letters addressed to demons on his desk, pledging ritual blood sacrifice in return for granting his wishes.

When Danyal was arrested, police noted cuts on both of his hands. His DNA was obtained and tested against the DNA from the crime scene, and it was a match.

As his trial started, the evidence painted a haunting picture of Danyal Hussein's sinister intentions. Surveillance footage captured Danyal at an ASDA store purchasing the knives that would be used to murder Bibba and Nicole and presumably other women. The court learned of Danyal's obsession with the lottery. He had a twisted belief that sacrificing women would lead him to a winning jackpot.

Members of the court were shown the blood-signed document with the demon Danyal called Lucifuge Rofocale. The agreement promised to sacrifice six women every six months to appease the demon and enhance his chances of winning the Mega Millions Super Jackpot lottery.

Danyal denied all charges and had a defiant demeanor throughout the trial, but the overwhelming evidence left the jury with no doubt. They found him guilty of the double murder.

Mrs. Justice Whipple handed Danyal a 35-year prison sentence, saying,

---

"You committed these vicious attacks. You did it to kill. You did it for money and a misguided pursuit of power. This was a calculated and deliberate course of conduct, planned and carried out with precision.

Bizarre though the pact with the devil may appear to others, this was your belief system, your own commitment to the murder of innocent women. No family should have to endure this."

Mina Smallman, the mother of Nicole and Bibaa was an archdeacon in the Church of England. She says she has forgiven the man responsible for her daughters' murders. She told the UK newspaper, *The Sun*, "It's about being able to hear beyond the evil of this world. You have to dig deep when the bad times come. Finding my faith has saved me on numerous occasions, and at times like this, you need it."

This case was followed across the UK not just because of the heinous nature of the murders but because two Metropolitan Police officers, Deniz Jaffer, and Jamie Lewis, were sentenced to 33 months imprisonment each for capturing and disseminating unsuitable images of the sisters' remains at the scene of the crime.

These photographs were taken on the night of June 8th, where the bodies were found and were shared in various WhatsApp groups. One of the officers even modified an image by adding his own face to it, creating a picture that resembled a selfie. These distasteful images were not only sent to fellow officers but also to individuals who were not part of the police force. Eventually, both Jaffer and Lewis were dismissed from their duties by the Metropolitan Police.

BLONDE, BLUE-EYED VIRGIN

On the evening of July 22nd, 1995, 15-year-old Elyse Pahler left her family home in Arroyo Grande, California. She told her parents she was heading out to spend time with friends. The three boys she was meeting were not really her friends but acquaintances. The group's agenda for the evening involved smoking marijuana in a secluded eucalyptus grove nearby. What Elyse didn't know is that the boys had orchestrated the outing with a sinister purpose—to murder her because they thought she resembled the Virgin Mary. They intended to offer Elyse as a sacrifice to the devil.

The boys, Royce Casey, Jacob Delashmutt, and Joseph Fiorella, were all between the ages of 14 and 16. They were members of a local heavy metal band called Hatred. As they all sat smoking outside, the influence of marijuana lowered Elyse's guard. As she relaxed, Casey, Delashmutt, and Fiorella set their plan in motion. Casey held Elyse down while Delashmutt used his belt to choke her. Fiorella pulled out a hunting knife and started stabbing Elyse in the neck. Each boy took turns stabbing her, and in her last moments, Elyse was on the ground, crying for God and her mother as she bled to death. In an incomprehensible act hours later, each boy sexually assaulted Elyse's corpse in the silent eucalyptus grove.

The three boys were fascinated by heavy metal music and drawn to its darker elements. Fixated on the Satanism and sacrificial themes in the group Slayer's song lyrics, they were convinced that performing a sacrifice would give them power and help their own band, Hatred, become famous.

Elyse's body remained undiscovered for eight months before one of her murderers, Royce Casey, told police where her body could be found. Her body was in an advanced state of decomposition but still bore the signs of her horrifying death. Casey said he confessed because of his recent conversion to Christianity. He felt that Delashmutt and Fiorella would kill again and may even try to kill him.

The three teenagers were arrested and pleaded no contest when confronted with their charges. During the trial, Casey's confession was read, which revealed the twisted ideology that had driven the boys to select Elyse as their victim. They thought she was the epitome of purity and innocence—a young girl known for her blonde hair and blue eyes —a virgin untouched by life's vices. To them, she was the ultimate sacrificial offering.

The court handed down sentences ranging from 26 years in prison to life imprisonment with the possibility of parole. Their sentencing, however, brought little solace to the Pahler family, who had to live with the reality that their daughter had been taken away from them violently and senselessly.

Elyse's parents, David and Lisanne Pahler filed a lawsuit against the band Slayer in 2001. They alleged that Slayer's lyrics had contributed to their daughter's murder and that Slayer's music was a harmful product. This case joined a list of historical cases where artists faced lawsuits due to their fans' actions. The judge dismissed the lawsuit, stating that those who create music and other forms of creative expression can't be held legally accountable for the actions of those who consume it.

The Pahlers challenged the verdict, but the California Court of Appeal confirmed the dismissal in 2003. The appeals court also pointed out that a positive outcome for the Pahlers might inadvertently suppress free speech.

The Pahlers eventually became destitute and lost their home. Lisanne had trouble keeping a job, and the death of his daughter gave David PTSD. Years later, David was cut off in traffic and followed the driver to a parking lot. He dented their car door and pulled the driver out of the car. He was arrested and charged with a misdemeanor in 2013 in the road rage incident.

"For many months, we suffered through the nightmare of not knowing what happened to Elyse. When her body was finally discovered, I learned that she had been barbarically murdered, and I was consumed with grief. Although the defendants received prison sentences, it did little to ease the horror of what they'd done. The pain of losing my daughter and knowing she suffered will never leave me."

David Pahler, February 2017

Joseph Fiorella, now in his 40s, is incarcerated in High Desert State Prison in California. He has been eligible for parole since 2019 and has been denied release. Jacob Delashmutt, also in a California prison, is still incarcerated and has been eligible for parole since 2017.

Royce Casey is close to freedom. On March 17th, 2021, he was granted parole. Soon after, the San Luis Obispo County District Attorney's office asked California Governor Gavin Newsom to reverse the parole board's decision. In his parole review, Gov. Newsom said, "I have determined that Mr. Casey must do additional work to deepen his insight into the causative factors of his crime and coping skills before he can be safely released on parole."

The reversal didn't last long. A local superior court judge reversed Newsom's decision to deny Casey parole.

"After review of the record, the Court cannot find evidence to support the Governor's decision and, therefore, grants the requested relief and reinstates the Board's grant of parole."

Judge Craig Van Rooyen, June 6th, 2022

Casey's status still shows incarcerated in the California prison system, but with the judge's decree, he could be released anytime. Pahler's family doesn't oppose Casey's release. Through their lawyer, they made a statement.

"The family is prepared for Royce to be paroled. They know it is going to happen at some point. For the most part, the family is at peace with the decision. Royce has been generally an honor inmate. He's really tried to reform his life and make better of himself. Generally, there is no unanimity, but the family has accepted it."

BTK

Dennis Rader, commonly known as the BTK, is one of the most infamous serial killers in American history. Between 1974 and 1991, he was responsible for the murder of 10 people. His crimes were not just a result of sinister urges; they were the culmination of meticulous planning and rigorous mental and physical preparation before each kill.

Growing up, Dennis Rader's childhood seemed, on the surface, to be unremarkable. He participated in activities like the Boy Scouts of America and was an active member of the church youth group. Academically, Dennis was an average student.

Beneath this veneer of normalcy lurked a darker side. From a tender age, Rader harbored disturbing fantasies, often centered around bondage and the torture of women. Even more alarming was his secret penchant for killing and hanging small animals, a behavior often linked to future violent tendencies.

Rader's ability to maintain such a façade was a testament to his skill in deception. He wore the mask of normalcy so convincingly that those around him remained oblivious to his urges. Friends and neighbors described him as normal and polite. The idea that Rader could be responsible for such heinous acts was unfathomable to them.

By day, he was the friendly neighbor, the churchgoer, and the community member. By night, he was BTK, stalking his victims and planning his next act of violence. This duality allowed Rader to evade suspicion for years.

PREPARING TO KILL

Before committing his crimes, Rader adhered to a strict regime to ensure he was mentally and physically ready to commit murder. Rader reveled in the pre-planning process leading up to each kill. The moniker *BTK* is an acronym representing his chilling ritual: Bind, Torture, Kill, a moniker that Rader chose himself.

In the twisted world Rader inhabited, he saw himself as more than just a killer. He believed he was an undercover operative immersed in a deadly spy game. This fantasy was not just a mere daydream; it played a significant role in how he approached the murder of his victims.

RITUAL STALKING

His victims, whom he referred to as his *targets*, were unsuspecting individuals. Before the act, Rader would stalk the targets, observing their routines and daily habits. He would take notes as if gathering intelligence on an enemy agent. Once he had enough information, he would craft a detailed *kill plan* for each victim. In interviews after his arrest, Rader said these plans made him feel as though he was playing a high-stakes game, one that he had to win.

MURDER BLUEPRINTS

Rader had a blueprint for each murder, outlining every step to ensure his needs were met and the plan was executed without a hitch.

One of Rader's most unsettling preparations was the creation of his *murder kits.* These were pre-assembled collections of tools and items he believed essential for his acts. He stashed these kits in various locations, ensuring he always had access to his instruments of terror. Inside the kit, one could find an array of rubber gloves he used explicitly for strangulation, different kinds of knives, and ropes. He even sorted these tools based on the nature of his intended crime, distinguishing between tools for single murders and those for killing entire families.

Rader's planning wasn't just limited to his tools. His entire approach, from selecting a victim to ensuring he left no evidence behind, was methodical. He prided himself on thinking through every detail, every possible hiccup in his plan, and devising a solution well in advance. His crimes were chilling not just because of their brutality but also because of the cold, calculated planning that preceded them.

One of the most disturbing aspects of his planning was his choice of clothing. Rader assembled what could only be described as a dark wardrobe of *killing clothing*. These were not just outfits but costumes that played a pivotal role in his crimes. Every garment was carefully chosen to stoke the fires of his deranged fantasies, making each act even more gruesome in his eyes.

This theatrical approach went beyond mere clothing. Rader often set the stage for his crimes, ensuring the environment complemented the darkness of his actions. His victims were not just individuals to be harmed; they were actors in his twisted play, with Rader as the director, ensuring every scene played out to his macabre satisfaction.

VICTIM VULNERABILITY

Rader went to great lengths to ensure his victims felt utterly alone and vulnerable during their final moments. A crucial part of his strategy was to cut off any potential lifelines they might have to the outside world. He would disconnect the telephone wires to his victims' homes. He effectively severed their connection to the outside world by ensuring they couldn't reach out for assistance. This isolation was both a practical tactic to prevent them from calling for help and a psychological tool to heighten their fear and fuel his excitement.

THE OTERO FAMILY

On January 15th, around 8 am, Rader quietly made his way to the back of the Otero residence, where he cut the phone line. He entered the house through the back door and found the Otero family sitting inside, accompanied by a fiercely protective family dog.

Holding the family at gunpoint, Rader forced the father, Joe Otero, aged 38, to take the dog outside into the back-yard. He fabricated a story, claiming to be a wanted criminal on the run, needing food, money, and a vehicle. Rader directed the family to lie down in the living room before herding them into a bedroom. Believing that Rader's sole intention was robbery, the Otero family complied with his demand to be bound.

However, they soon realized their tragic mistake. Rader placed a bag over Joe Otero's head and used a cord to subdue and ultimately kill him. He then turned his attention to Joe's wife, Julie Otero, aged 34, attempting to strangle her with his bare hands. It took multiple attempts before he succeeded in ending her life.

Next, nine-year-old Joey Otero met a horrifying fate. He was discovered lifeless, facedown on his bedroom floor, suffocated with a bag over his head. Rader had even brought a chair into the room, positioning himself to watch the young child's agonizing death.

Eleven-year-old Josie Otero suffered an even more gruesome fate. Rader took her to the basement and hanged her by a noose tied around a sewer pipe. He callously left her partially naked, and later, investigators found evidence of semen on the pipe behind her lifeless body.

After committing these brutal murders, Rader meticulously cleaned the crime scene, taking a few souvenirs with him. He also fled in the Otero's station wagon, almost causing an accident while hastily backing out of the driveway. From there, he drove to a local supermarket, where a witness recalled seeing Rader exit the vehicle while visibly trembling. Rader tossed the car keys onto the market's rooftop, only then realizing he'd left a knife behind at the Otero residence. He returned to the house to retrieve the knife before making his getaway.

Unbeknownst to Rader, three other Otero children had already left for school before his arrival. Tragically, teenagers Charlie, Daniel, and Carmen returned home that day to a horrific nightmare.

After the Otero family murders, Rader recognized the importance of physical strength and endurance. It wasn't enough to have the intent; he needed the physical capability to murder. He started doing habitual hand exercises. Simple actions, like squeezing a ball repeatedly, were integral to his routine. These exercises were designed to ensure that his hands were powerful and ready for efficient strangulation.

KATHRYN BRIGHT

On the morning of April 4th, 1974, Rader broke into the home of 21-year-old Kathryn Bright. Concealing himself in her bedroom, he patiently awaited her arrival, accompanied by her 19-year-old brother Kevin, at 2 pm. They were abruptly confronted by a man emerging from the back room armed with a gun as they entered the house. Employing his usual methods, Rader bound Kathryn in her bedroom.

Kevin was taken to another room and restrained using available materials. Rader attempted to strangle Kevin with a stocking, but Kevin managed to break free momentarily and seize Rader's gun. A desperate struggle ensued, but Kevin received two gunshots to the head and face during the confrontation.

In a state of panic, Rader hurriedly attacked Kathryn, delivering deep stab wounds to her abdomen and other areas before fleeing the scene. Meanwhile, Kevin, though gravely injured, had feigned death and managed to escape the house and seek help.

He swiftly encountered two men on the street, and together, they rushed back to the scene. However, by the time they arrived, Rader had already vanished, leaving on foot to retrieve his parked car a few blocks away.

Kathryn Bright died from her injuries several hours later. Kevin survived the attack but sustained permanent injuries.

SHIRLEY VIAN

In March 1977, Rader allegedly targeted two homes but found them empty. Posing as a detective, he approached a five-year-old boy in the neighborhood, showing him a picture of his own wife and inquiring if the boy had seen her. He followed the child back to his house and gained entry when three other children there allowed him in. The oldest child was eight years old.

After drawing the shades and turning off the television, Rader's plan was suddenly interrupted when the mother,

24-year-old Shirley Vian, entered the room wearing her bathrobe. Rader promptly barricaded the children in the bathroom and proceeded to bind and strangle Shirley to death using a cord. He left the children unharmed in the confines of the bathroom. Forensic evidence later revealed seminal traces near Shirley's body.

NANCY FOX

In December of that year, Rader selected Nancy Fox, a 25-year-old jewelry store clerk, as his next victim. He gained entry to her vacant apartment through the bedroom window. He cut her phone line and patiently waited for her return. When Nancy Fox entered her apartment, she was startled to find an armed man waiting inside.

Complying with his orders, she undressed and allowed Rader to bind her to the bed. Once secured, Rader revealed his true identity as the perpetrator behind the recent murders, declaring her as his next victim. Rader strangled her to death, and again, semen was discovered on a nightgown near her lifeless body.

LETTER TO THE EDITOR

In early 1978, the Wichita Eagle received a postcard featuring a sarcastic poem entitled "Shirley Locks." Initially, its significance went unnoticed. However, days later, another letter followed, devoid of poetic flair. It directly claimed responsibility for the murders of the Otero family, Shirley Vain, and Nancy Fox.

The frustrated author expressed dissatisfaction with the media's coverage of the murders. Wichita police publicized the information, alerting the community to the presence of a serial killer in their peaceful town. Citizens were urged to be vigilant, lock doors and windows, and check for a dial tone on their phones upon entering their homes.

ANNA WILLIAMS

Anna Williams, a recently widowed 63-year-old woman, found herself unknowingly on the brink of becoming the next victim of BTK. It was April of 1979 when Rader broke into Anna's home. He carefully rummaged through her personal belongings and couldn't resist taking a few small items as macabre mementos of his intrusion. However, he had to leave before Anna returned home.

Two months passed, and Anna received an unexpected package in the mail. Its contents sent chills down her spine. Inside was a poem titled "Oh Anna, Why Didn't You Appear," a haunting reminder that BTK had set his sights on her. Terrified, Anna made a quick decision to flee the area, leaving the state of Kansas behind in hopes of escaping the clutches of the predator.

The package sent to Anna was not an isolated incident. Another package, bearing a similar poem, arrived at the doorstep of KAKE-TV.

The poem revealed the sick and twisted mindset of the killer. It spoke of deviant pleasure, the awakening of a new season, and the intertwining of fear, longing, and desperation. The words painted a grotesque picture of a predator reveling in the torment and suffering of his victims. Anna, along with the rest of the community, could not escape the chilling realization that an insidious monster was hunting them.

BTK seemed to vanish from the public eye for the next 15 years. The community and police wondered if the killer had died.

MARINE HEDGE

In April 1985, Rader resurfaced, driven again by his insatiable urges. This time, his target was Marine Hedge, a 53-year-old widow living just half a mile from his home. Rader meticulously planned his attack, using his role as a scout leader to create an alibi. He slipped away while attending a Boy Scout camp with his son, claiming a sudden headache.

Rader broke into Marine's house, severing the phone line to ensure she couldn't call for help. To his disappointment, she was not home at the time. Undeterred, he hid in her bedroom closet, waiting patiently for her return. Hours passed until finally, Marine and a male friend entered the house. Rader bided his time until the friend left, leaving Marine alone in the darkness of her bedroom.

When the moment was right, Rader emerged from the closet. He overpowered her, forcefully strangling her on the bed. Unsatisfied with just the act of murder, Rader dragged Marine's lifeless body, along with the bedding, to her car. He transported her to his church, where he had unrestricted access. He meticulously posed her body in the basement, taking photographs to savor the event.

Once he had photos, Rader disposed of Marine's body in a shallow grave outside Park City. He meticulously wiped down any traces of his presence before returning to the Boy Scout camp, his façade of normalcy firmly intact.

VICKI WEGERLE

Vicki Wegerle became the next victim. In September 1986, he arrived at her doorstep disguised as a telephone repairman. Vicki, unsuspecting, let him into her home. Rader wasted no time in overpowering her, binding her, and subjecting her to his twisted fantasies. He strangled her and documented the act with photographs that would serve as his trophies.

When Vicki's husband returned home and discovered the unimaginable scene, he was devastated. The police, initially suspecting him, compounded his grief. Innocent and wrongly questioned, he was subjected to the anguish of being a murder suspect while mourning the loss of his beloved wife.

DOLORES DAVIS

In 1991, Rader turned his attention to Dolores Davis, a 62-year-old woman living alone near his home. Rader smashed through Dolores' sliding glass door, gaining access to her home. Finding her reading in bed, he concocted a story about being a vagrant needing money, lulling her into a false sense of security. But his intentions were far from innocent. He bound her, rendering her helpless, before tightening his grip around her throat, extinguishing her life.

For years, the horrors perpetrated by BTK remained unsolved. However, a renewed interest in these crimes was sparked by the efforts of Robert Beattie, a Wichita lawyer deeply invested in the case. Determined to bring attention back to these unsolved atrocities, Beattie authored a book. The book and the media coverage it garnered thrust BTK back into the public consciousness in early 2003. The resurgence of interest in the case was not lost on Dennis Rader. Unable to resist the allure of the spotlight and perhaps perturbed by the renewed scrutiny, Rader began to communicate once more. He sent chilling packages and letters to media outlets and law enforcement, taunting them with details of the crimes known only to the killer.

His communications were a mix of arrogance and a desire to control the narrative surrounding his crimes. But while Rader believed he was outsmarting everyone, he was unwittingly setting the stage for his capture. The reign of BTK, which had spanned decades, was finally drawing to a close. Despite Rader's attempts to taunt and mislead investigators with his communications, his arrogance proved to be his undoing.

In February 2005, Rader sent a floppy disk to the Fox TV affiliate, KSAS-TV, in Wichita. This disk contained a Microsoft Word document with writings from BTK. However, when police IT specialists analyzed the disk, they found residual data from a previously deleted Microsoft Word document that Rader had overlooked. This hidden information pointed to the Christ Lutheran Church, where Rader was employed. Detectives identified the last individual to edit the document as someone named *Dennis*. A swift online search revealed that Dennis Rader served as the Christ Lutheran Church council president. They'd found their killer.

The community breathed a sigh of relief when the man responsible for so much pain and terror was taken into custody.

The sentencing proceedings offered the victims' families

a platform to confront the man who had wreaked havoc on their lives. In a courtroom charged with emotions ranging from grief to anger, family members faced Rader, seeking closure and justice.

On August 18th, 2005, Rader received a sentence of at least 175 years with no possibility of parole. This was the maximum sentence permissible, as Kansas did not have a death penalty in place at that time.

Now 78 years old, Rader resides at the El Dorado Correctional Facility in Kansas.

A STUDIED KILLER

On February 1st, 2012, Samantha Koenig, an 18-year-old, vanished during her shift at the Common Grounds coffee kiosk in Anchorage, Alaska. Samantha had just given a man in a ski mask his coffee order when he pulled out a gun and yelled at her to hand over the money from the register, which she promptly did.

Barging into the kiosk after the initial confrontation, the man zip-tied Samantha's hands and tried to force her into his truck. She attempted to escape and got away for a moment, but the man tackled her and threatened to shoot her. The man informed Samantha that she was a victim of a ransom kidnapping. He promised he wouldn't hurt her if she cooperated.

The man had prepared his truck ahead of time for the kidnapping by removing the license plate and the tool-boxes attached to the truck bed. After securing Samantha inside the truck, he drove off with his captive.

The man locked Samantha in a shed situated in front of his own house. She was still restrained, and he turned on the radio so nearby neighbors wouldn't hear her scream. He told her to stay quiet and that he owned a police scanner and would know if she tried to notify the neighbors.

The man drove to the coffee kiosk where Samatha had left her phone. He accessed the cell phone and sent a deceptive text to her boyfriend, suggesting that she had had a bad day and decided to hang out with friends for the weekend. He went back to the shed and demanded Samantha's debit card. She told him that she and her boyfriend had a joint bank account, and his ATM card was located in the truck they both used. She gave him directions to her boyfriend's house and the PIN for the card.

The man drove to the boyfriend's home and grabbed the ATM card from his truck. While there, Samantha's boyfriend, who thought the man was a burglar, confronted him, shouted at him, and ran into his house to call the police. The man left the vicinity before he could be found. He then drove to an ATM to verify the PIN Samantha had given him. Afterward, he went back to the shed. He sexually assaulted Samantha and stran- gled her to death. He left her body in the shed for 16 days while he went on a cruise that left from New Orleans.

When he came back, he constructed a ransom note, but

before he sent it, he went into the shed and posed Samantha's body so she looked alive. He stapled her eyes open and applied some makeup to her face. He photographed her alongside a recent newspaper for proof of life. The photograph was paired with a demand for $30,000 to be deposited in Samantha's bank account. Using Samantha's phone, the man contacted her boyfriend with directions to the photo and ransom note which the man had left in a local park.

The man cut a hole in nearby Matanuska Lake and discarded Samantha's dismembered body. Meanwhile, the community, misled by the false evidence of life in the photograph, banded together to provide the ransom money, which Samantha's father deposited into her shared account.

The money was withdrawn in four states and was tracked by authorities. Through careful analysis of the available details, authorities started tracking a white Ford Focus associated with withdrawals in Texas. Before they could locate the individual in the car, the man was pulled over for a routine traffic stop in Texas. The Texas State Trooper was suspicious and searched the man's car. A ski mask, firearm, and Samantha's phone were found. The man was arrested and was finally on his way to paying for his crimes. The trooper who arrested him didn't know that he'd just arrested serial killer Israel Keyes, who had been on a criminal rampage for 16 years. Samantha Koenig was his final victim.

EARLY YEARS

Israel Keyes was born in Richmond, Utah, on January 7th, 1978. His parents, Heidi and Jeff Keyes, welcomed him as the second of their ten children. The Keyes family was initially associated with The Fundamentalist Church of Jesus Christ of Latter-Day Saints in Torrance, California.

From birth until 1983, Keyes and his siblings received homeschooling rooted in Christian teachings. After the family's departure from the FLDS church, they relocated to a remote area north of Colville, Washington, in Stevens County. The Keyes family lived in a one-room cabin on Rocky Creek Road, lacking modern amenities like electricity or running water.

While in Colville, the family joined a church known as the Ark, which aligned itself with the Christian Identity ideology known for its white supremacist beliefs. The church taught its members that sexual relations between different races was a sin.

Due to the limited space in their cabin, many of the Keyes siblings were forced to sleep outdoors. Their survival depended on hunting, gathering firewood, and working on neighboring farms. Keyes, in particular, was known for his indiscriminate hunting and once shared how he skinned a deer while it was still alive with fellow church members, leading to his ostracization.

By his mid-teens, Keyes had developed his carpentry skills and built a cabin for his family at 16. He also spent two years working for a contractor in Colville. He kept a journal from his younger days, frequently referencing biblical verses and expressing remorse over perceived sins. The family later relocated to Smyrna, Maine, integrating into an Amish community and engaging in maple syrup production. Their mother's religious strictness meant that the children had to covertly participate in recreational activities like watching films and were forbidden from learning musical instruments for religious reasons.

After a particularly intense argument where Keyes expressed his atheistic views, his parents distanced him from the family and told his brothers and sisters to have no contact with him. Keyes's interests shifted towards occult practices, and he reportedly contemplated a ritualistic murder. Eventually, Keyes dissociated from his former religious beliefs.

JULIE MARIE HARRIS

Julie Marie Harris, a 13-year-old Special Olympics medal recipient for skiing, disappeared while waiting for a ride to a church in Colville, Washington, on March 2nd, 1996. Her remains were discovered in a wooded area several miles from her initial location over a year later, on April 26, 1997. The exact cause of death remains unknown. Notably, Harris was a double amputee, and her prosthetic feet were found by the Colville River approximately a month after her disappearance. At the time, an 18-year-old Keyes lived nearby. After his arrest in 2012, he was questioned regarding Harris's case, but he neither confirmed nor denied involvement.

Around the same time, another incident in Colville involved 12-year-old Cassandra "Cassie" Emerson, who was reported missing after her mother, Marlene Kay Emerson, aged 29, was found in their fire-damaged trailer home on June 27th, 1997. Cassie's remains were found in 1998, approximately thirteen miles from her home. Keyes confessed to initiating a fire in a trailer in Colville, marking his first known arson event.

MILITARY CAREER

On July 9th, 1998, Keyes enlisted in the United States Army in New York State. He was designated a Specialist within Alpha Company, 1st Battalion, 5th Infantry Regiment. His postings included assignments at Fort Lewis and Fort Hood, with overseas duties in Sinai, Egypt. While in Sinai, he reportedly told a fellow soldier he wanted to kill him.

After an honorable discharge, Keyes settled in Neah Bay, Washington, within the Makah Reservation community on the Olympic Peninsula. In 2007, Keyes ventured into the construction sector in Alaska, founding Keyes

Construction and undertaking roles such as a handyman and contractor.

MODUS OPERANDI

Keyes evaded capture for years, partly due to his keen understanding of other infamous criminals and their methods. Unlike many criminals who operate impulsively, Keyes undertook extensive research into the crimes, methods, and shortcomings of other notorious serial killers. This study fueled his dark interests and provided insights into evading capture. Many serial killers fall into routines or develop a signature modus operandi, which often becomes their undoing. Keyes studied these patterns and deliberately avoided establishing any consistent methods. He varied his choice of victims, killing techniques, and crime locations.

He often planned the murders for extended periods and preferred isolated areas and campgrounds. Although he claimed a reluctance to use firearms, after speaking with him, law enforcement thought his preference for strangulation originated from his desire to watch his victims struggle. Despite saying that he didn't kill children, police and FBI personnel suspect his involvement in the deaths of several minors and adolescents.

According to an FBI document, between 2001 and 2012, Keyes is believed to have burglarized between twenty to thirty homes nationwide and robbed multiple banks. He is implicated in 11 murders within the U.S., with the possibility of more overseas.

Keyes stood out for his unparalleled preparation. He buried his murder kits – a disturbing mix of money, weapons, and tools – sometimes years before he would commit a crime. This foresight allowed him to act without the burden of transporting incriminating items during his travels.

When talking with police, Keyes occasionally drew parallels between his actions and other serial killers, either underscoring his perceived superior methods or highlighting mistakes he easily avoided. He would typically commit his crimes away from his home, ensuring no two incidents occurred in the same vicinity. He exercised considerable caution during these excursions — turning off his mobile device and transacting solely in cash. He maintained no known ties to his victims. One incident involved Keyes traveling from Chicago to Vermont—a distance of 1,000 miles (1,600 kilometers)—after which he used a previously stashed *murder kit* to execute the crime.

THE BOCA KILLER

Keyes is also a person of interest in a series of crimes in 2007 near Boca Raton, Florida, linked to the so-called *Boca Killer*. The first incident involved Randi Ann Malitz Gorenberg, 52, who was abducted on March 23rd, 2007, from the Boca Town Center Mall parking lot. Within an hour of this event, her body, with fatal gunshot wounds, was found at another location. On August 7th, 2007, a woman and her young son were abducted from the same mall. The perpetrator hid his identity with a mask and sunglasses. Still, the victim caught brief glimpses of his appearance, which she described as consistent with a photograph of Israel Keyes. This victim was eventually released unharmed after she was forced to withdraw cash from an ATM. The third incident involved the tragic deaths of Nancy Bochicchio, 47, and her daughter, Joey Bochicchio-Hauser, 7. Their bodies were found with fatal gunshot wounds in their car at the Boca Town Center Mall parking lot on December 12th, 2007.

Israel Keyes confessed to the homicides of William "Bill" Scott Currier, 49, and his wife, Lorraine Simonne Currier, 55, residents of Essex, Vermont. On the night of June 8th, 2011, Keyes forcefully entered their home, restrained the couple, and transported them to an abandoned farmhouse. In this isolated location, he shot Bill before assaulting and strangling Lorraine. Despite ongoing investigations, their remains remain undiscovered. Intriguingly, two years before the incident, Keyes had hidden a *murder kit* near the Currier residence. After the homicides, he moved the kit to Parishville, New York, where it stayed concealed until his capture.

While in custody, on May 23rd, 2012, Keyes made a failed escape attempt during a routine legal proceeding by using wood shavings from a pencil to free himself from restraints. Officers swiftly responded, restraining him with a Taser.

While under arrest for charges related to the Koenig murder, Keyes committed suicide at the Anchorage Correctional Complex. Despite strict supervision that only permitted the use of an electric razor, he managed to hide a traditional razor blade. On December 2nd, 2012, he died from wrist lacerations and attempted self-strangulation. Under his remains, authorities found a note— a chilling poetic homage to murder— yet it brought no new leads on potential victims. In 2020, the FBI disclosed drawings found posthumously in Keyes's cell, drawn in blood, featuring eleven skulls and a penta-gram. One specific drawing bore the phrase "WE ARE ONE" at its base. Authorities speculate that the number of skulls might represent Keyes's total victim count.

BUTCHER OF ROSTOV

In 1990, Andrei Chikatilo was apprehended and found guilty of the murders of over 52 children and adults in the Soviet Union. Andrei primarily preyed on young women and children, often engaging with them at train stations. He lured them away from transportation hubs with money, alcohol, toys, and candy. His ritual was usually the same each time. He would lead them to a secluded woodland area or shed, restrain them, and stab them to achieve sexual release.

Andrei's crimes were brutal, and he often mutilated his victims in various ways. He gouged out his victim's eyes because he thought police would be able to see his image in their eyes. He danced around his victims with his knife, stabbing them in the stomach and biting off their noses. He earned his nickname, *The Butcher of Rostov*.

EARLY TRAUMA

Andrei was born on October 16th, 1936, in the Ukrainian SSR, which was then part of the Soviet Union. His childhood was marked by the harsh realities of Soviet rural life during the great Ukrainian famine in the early 1930s. Raised in a one-room hut, Andrei was frequently told about the death of an older brother, Stepan, who was kidnapped and cannibalized by starving neighbors. This story painted a grim picture of the world for the young Andrei, and he learned early on to fear and distrust others. The devastation of the famine, combined with the political climate of Stalin's rule, cast a dark shadow over the boy's formative years.

In 1943, Andrei's mother had a daughter named Tatyana. Andrei's father was away fighting in WWII and wasn't Tatyana's father. Ukrainian women faced sexual assault from German soldiers during the war, and Tatyana was likely a product of that assault. Since Andrei and his mother shared a one-room dwelling, it's possible that Andrei was present when it happened.

As a child, Andrei suffered from hydrocephalus, also called water-on-the-brain. The extra water can cause brain damage, and Andrei suffered from urinary incontinence. While his father was away, he and his mother shared a single bed. Andrei frequently wet the bed, for which his mother would scold and beat him. At home, Andrei and his sister faced regular reprimands from their mother. His sister, Tatyana, later described their father as a gentle soul, unlike their strict and unsympathetic mother.

In September 1944, at age eight, Andrei started school. He was introverted and also physically frail. He suffered from malnutrition and wore handmade clothes to school. The malnutrition occasionally caused him to collapse both at home and in school, and he was bullied because of his small size and evident poverty.

As he reached adolescence, Andrei discovered that he had chronic impotence, an issue that further isolated him from his peers and deeply affected his self-esteem. As Andrei transitioned into his teenage years, the scars of his traumatic childhood became more pronounced in his behavior and interactions. His only sexual experience came at age 17 when he was wrestling with an 11-year-old girl who was his sister's friend. He pinned the girl down and ejaculated as the girl struggled to escape his grasp.

Later that year, he started a relationship with a young woman; however, he still struggled with erectile dysfunction during their attempts at intimacy. The relationship lasted a little over a year. His sexual dysfunction became common knowledge among his friends and acquaintances, and he later confessed that he felt everyone was discussing his condition behind his back. This drove him to an unsuccessful suicide attempt.

Following this incident, he left his birthplace and relocated to Rostov-on-Don.

ADULT LIFE

In 1963, two weeks after they met, Andrei married Feodosia Odnacheva. They had almost no intimate life but were able to have two children, Lyudmila and Yuri, through manual insemination. During the 1970s, he earned a degree in literature by correspondence from the University of Rostov. He started to work as a teacher of Russian language and literature. His teaching style was awkward, and he could not maintain control of his students, who, in turn, bullied him.

THE KILLING YEARS

This period became a turning point in Andrei's life. Andrei sexually assaulted several children at the school. His modus operandi included hurting them in some manner, like slamming them against a wall; only then was he able to achieve a sexual release. He was a voyeur in the restrooms and the school dormitories as well. Andrei was forced to resign from his teaching position when parents complained, but he was never formally charged with sexual assault. This didn't deter him. He got a teaching position at another school in Rostov-on-Don and purchased a secret house nearby where he would commit many of his murders.

On December 22nd, 1978, Andrei committed his first confirmed murder; he enticed Lena Zakotnova, a nine-year-old girl, into a deserted shed with the promise of imported candy. He tried to sexually assault the girl but was unable to do so. She was fighting and screaming, and although he tried to strangle her, he failed. He stabbed her several times to subdue her, creating a sexual release for him. He now knew that extreme violence would allow him sexual gratification, and this became the goal of his future murders. He dumped Lena's body in a river while she was still alive, and her body was found two days later.

Police initially thought Andrei was a suspect because a local woman, Svetlana Gurenkova, said she saw Lena with a man who matched Andrei's description. She said a man wearing a long black overcoat, with gray hair and glasses, walked up to the young girl and started speaking with her. Andrei was questioned but never charged because his wife gave him a solid alibi.

His second murder was three years later and was more gruesome than the first. Seventeen-year-old Larisa Tkachenko was lured from a bus stop into the forest with the promise of vodka and food. She was sexually experienced and had traded food for sex before with soldiers. Once in the woods, Andrei ripped the girl's clothes off and tried unsuccessfully to sexually assault her. Larisa fought him and screamed, so he stuffed dirt in her mouth to keep her from screaming. Because he had no knife with him, he ended up strangling her. He stabbed and sexually assaulted her with a stick and bit off chunks of her flesh. When he was finished, Andrei covered Larisa's body with dirt and leaves. She was found the next day. Larisa Tkachenko's murder was brutal, and Andrei now knew that even without a knife, he could create enough violence for his sexual release. He now had a firm pattern of behavior.

Andrei's routine now included trolling train stations and bus stops for young girls and boys he could lure to his secret house or into the forest with candy or alcohol. He also murdered adult women who worked as sex workers or were homeless. He committed dozens of murders this way. The victims were usually mutilated with a knife which he used as a penis substitute. He also removed body parts, often sex organs, and engaged in cannibalism with the body parts.

During the 1980s, serial killers were unheard of in the Soviet Union. Any evidence of serial murders or child abuse was concealed by the state-controlled media to maintain public order. As the number of victims increased, speculations about foreign conspiracies and werewolf assaults gained traction, leading to heightened public fear and curiosity despite the media's silence on the issue.

Fifteen more victims were found in 1984, and police focused their efforts on local transportation hubs. During this time, Andrei was apprehended for suspicious behavior at a bus station. He was released because his blood type did not align with the suspect's profile. His blood type, which was type A, differed from that found in his other bodily fluids (type AB). He was part of a rare group known as "non-secretors," in whom blood type can only be determined through a blood sample. Since the police only had a semen sample from the crime scenes and not the killer's blood, Andrei managed to elude the police.

The police finally arrested Andrei on November 20th, 1990, after he was seen at the train station acting suspiciously. He refused to confess to any of the murders. The police officer in charge of the case let a psychiatrist speak with Andrei. He opened up to the psychiatrist, offering exhaustive details about all his murders. He even took police to the locations of bodies that had not been found.

Andrei claimed he murdered 56 individuals, although only 53 could be confirmed independently. This number greatly surpassed the 36 victims the police had originally associated with their serial killer.

Andrei Chikatilo was tried in 1992 for 53 murders and five charges of sexual assault on minors. On October 15th, 1992, he was found guilty of 52 out of the 53 murders, and for each murder, he was sentenced to death. His total sentence amounted to the death penalty plus an additional 86 years.

Russia's president, Boris Yeltsin, refused Andrei's appeal

for clemency while on death row. On February 14th, 1994, Andrei, then age 57, was taken from his cell in Novocherkassk prison to a soundproofed room. He was executed with a single gunshot to his head behind his right ear. He was later buried in an anonymous grave within the prison cemetery.

No one could have predicted the magnitude of the atrocities that Andrei would commit. How many children and adults *The Butcher of Rostov* killed remains unknown.

BLOOD IN THE GREEN RIVER

In the summer of 1982, the bodies of five women were found in the Green River in King County, Washington. These grisly discoveries sparked a nationwide manhunt as authorities realized they were on the trail of one of America's most prolific serial killers.

The first of these bodies was found on July 15th, 1982, by two boys biking along the Green River in Kent, Washington. They noticed something odd below a bridge they were crossing. On closer inspection, they realized it was the body of a naked woman lying against one of the bridge's pilings. She appeared to have something around her neck.

The victim was quickly identified as sixteen-year-old Wendy Lee Coffield. She was last seen on July 8th, 1982, leaving her foster home in Tacoma, Washington. She was one of many young women who worked as a sex worker along the Pacific Highway South (PHS). Her autopsy showed that she died from strangulation and also suffered a broken arm before she died.

Less than a month later, on August 12th, the Green River revealed another victim. Debra Lynn Bonner, aged 23, was found floating naked and lifeless near the Kent slaughterhouse. She had been missing since July 25th and was also a sex worker who frequented *The Strip*, another name for the PHS. The horror didn't end there. Three days later, on August 15th, three more bodies were discovered. The victims, also known sex workers, were identified as Marcia Chapman, 31, Cynthia Hinds, 17, and Opal Mills, 16. Chapman and Hinds were found together in the water, and Mills was on the river bank nearby. Police were able to collect and preserve semen samples from Chapman and Hinds, but there was no DNA database in 1982. All of the women suffered a strangulation death.

As the body count rose, panic spread across Washington. The police realized they'd found the dumping ground of a serial murderer. The media quickly nicknamed the perpetrator *The Green River Killer*. The pattern of the murders, the victims' profiles, and the consistent method of strangulation left little doubt Washington state was dealing with a prolific serial killer. In the coming months and years, the hunt for the *Green River Killer* would become one of the most extensive and challenging investigations in American criminal history.

THE GREEN RIVER KILLER

Gary Leon Ridgway, later known as the *Green River Killer*, was born on February 18th, 1949, in Salt Lake City, Utah. While his name would go on to become synonymous with a chilling series of 48+ murders, there was little in his early life that foreshadowed the darkness to come.

Ridgway was born as the middle son to parents Mary and Thomas Ridgway. His father, Thomas, was often a peripheral figure in his upbringing. In contrast, his mother, Mary, was dominant in his life. Mary's influence on her son was profound. She was known for her strict, at times bordering on abusive, approach to parenting. Particularly disturbing was her reaction to Gary's bed-wetting episodes during his childhood. Her choice to wash him personally after each incident might have planted the seeds of the conflicting emotions of anger and attraction he felt toward her. Such a tumultuous mother-son relationship could have set the stage for his distorted view of women later in life.

The Ridgway home was far from serene. There were constant financial constraints and arguments between Ridgway's parents. Thomas Ridgway had a disdain for sex workers, which he openly discussed with his sons. This might have sown early seeds of contempt for sex workers in Gary's mind.

e Ridgway family decided to relo-
gton. This region, characterized
d the meandering Green River,
the haunting backdrop for Ridg-

EARLY BEHAVIORS

Ridgway also had violent tendencies from a young age.
Around the age of 16, he led a six-year-old boy into the
woods and stabbed him through the ribs. The boy
survived and remembered the incident, and Ridgway
later said he did it for no other reason than the thrill.

His academic performance stayed below average
throughout his school years. Ridgway attended Tyee
High School in SeaTac, Washington, where he struggled
with reading. He had undiagnosed dyslexia and an IQ in
the low 80s.

After graduating high school in 1969, Ridgway joined
the U.S. Navy and served for two years. While in the
service, he was stationed overseas and began frequenting
sex workers. He contracted gonorrhea yet continued to
engage in unprotected sex. This behavior would
continue when he returned to the U.S. and eventually
become intertwined with his decades-long murders.

MARRIAGES

Ridgway was married three times. His second wife later recounted troubling behaviors during their relationship, including his penchant for strangulation during intimate moments. His third wife, however, didn't observe any overt signs of his murderous activities, although she did note his obsession with sex. Both his first and second marriages ended due to unfaithfulness from both parties.

His second wife, Marcia Winslow, reported that Ridgway once tried to kill her during their marriage. However, he later underwent a religious transformation. This change saw him evangelizing door-to-door, reciting the Bible at work and home, and urging Marcia to strictly adhere to their pastor's teachings. Winslow said he would often become emotional during religious activities, shedding tears during sermons or when reading the Bible. However, Ridgway's newfound faith did not prevent him from seeking out sex workers. He also required Marcia to engage in public sex acts, occasionally in areas where he later dumped his victims.

Those close to Ridgway described him as having an overwhelming sexual urge. All three of his ex-wives and many past partners claimed he required sex multiple times daily. Ridgway said he disliked sex workers, even though he sought them out to fulfill his own needs.

JUDITH MAWSON

In 1985, Ridgway started dating Judith Mawson and married her in 1988. When Mawson moved into Ridgeway's home, she noted an absence of carpeting. After Ridgway's capture, law enforcement thought Ridgway might have used his carpet to wrap victims. Mawson told police that Ridgway usually left early for work to earn overtime. She wondered if he had used these early hours to commit his murders. Mawson asserted that she was unaware of Ridgway's activities and was unfamiliar with the term *Green River Killer* because she didn't watch the news.

Ridgeway murdered three women when he was married to Mawson, and in a jailhouse interview with author Pennie Morehead, he professed genuine affection for her. Mawson stated in an interview with the media, "I believe I've contributed to saving lives by being his spouse and bringing joy to his life."

For nearly 30 years, Ridgway worked at the Kenworth Truck Company in Renton, Washington, painting trucks. His colleagues described him as a good worker. As they saw it, nothing in his demeanor suggested he was capable of the dozens of murders he was committing in his free time.

MURDERS

During the two decades spanning the 1980s and 1990s, it is possible that Gary Ridgway was responsible for the deaths of 71 young women and teenagers in Washington state. Most of the murders were perpetrated between 1982 and 1984.

Ridgway later admitted in court testimonies that he murdered so many women that he struggled to keep an accurate tally. Many victims were either involved in sex work or were runaways whom Ridgway approached along the highway.

Ridgway would display a photograph of his son to these women as a ploy to gain their trust. After engaging in sex, usually from behind, Ridgway would choke the woman to death using his forearm. He would use his other arm to help him pull back until they stopped breathing. The murders occurred in his home, truck, and wooded areas. After the murder, Ridgway often performed the ritual of posing the women suggestively. He would sometimes return to where he dumped the body and to have sex with the corpse. He told police after his capture that this was a practical move since he wanted sex several times a day. He disliked the act of necrophilia and eventually began burying the bodies to help him resist the temptation. The remains of most of his victims were discovered in forested regions near the

Green River close to the Seattle–Tacoma International Airport. Other bodies were found in the southern part of King County, Washington.

In 2001, suspicions surrounding the deaths of four women led to the arrest of Gary Ridgway. Subsequent DNA analysis confirmed his connection to these victims. Further forensic examinations detected the presence of a specific spray paint identical to the type Ridgway used in his workplace at multiple crime scenes. These findings expanded the charges to include many additional murders.

Gary Ridgway admitted to more verified killings than any other serial killer in U.S. history. The police initially had 42 murders attributed to *The Green River Killer*, but Ridgway told them about 48 murders.

On November 5th, 2003, Gary Ridgway pleaded guilty to 48 counts of aggravated first-degree murder. This plea was part of an agreement, ensuring he would avoid the death penalty in return for his assistance in identifying the locations of his victims' remains. In the statement tied to his guilty plea, Ridgway clarified that all the murders occurred within King County, Washington. He also admitted to relocating and discarding the remains of two women near Portland as a tactic to mislead law enforcement.

Currently in his 70s and serving 48 life sentences,

Ridgway is incarcerated at the Washington State Penitentiary in Walla Walla, Washington. He will die in prison.

SERIAL BLACK MAGIC

Ahmad Suradji was a highly respected 48-year-old witch doctor in Medan, Indonesia. Many individuals confided in him for guidance on love, money, and health issues. Sorcerers are common in Indonesia; some even have shops in shopping malls. Ahmad worked his magic from his home near his sugar cane plantation. However, beneath the veneer of this revered mystic was a sinister secret that compelled him to commit ritual murder.

On the 24th of April 1997, Sri Kemala Dewi, a 21-year-old woman, asked a rickshaw driver named Andreas to take her to a place called *Datuk*. She asked Andreas not to tell anyone about her journey. She never requested a return pick-up. Three days later, a local man discovered Dewi's unclothed and decomposing remains on a sugarcane plantation. A crowd of residents exhumed the body and alerted authorities. The sugarcane plantation belonged to Ahmad Suradji. This chilling find sparked a police investigation that unveiled a horrific killing spree that had gone on for 11 years.

Ahmad's victims were primarily women seeking his aid to improve their wealth, health, and sexual desirability. They wanted him to use his magic to make their husbands faithful or help them conceive. A significant proportion of the women murdered were also sex workers. The victims, ranging from 11 to 30 years old, perhaps felt too embarrassed to disclose their consultations with the sorcerer to their families, so their disappearances remained unlinked to him.

Ahmad's modus operandi involved charging each victim based on their unique needs, typically between $200 and $400. After collecting the fee, he would lead them to a sugarcane plantation near his residence and partially bury them as part of the ritual. The women complied with this request, not realizing they would soon be murdered. Once they were immobilized, he strangled each woman with an electrical cable, drank their saliva, and undressed their corpses. After some time, he would remove the bodies from his sugarcane fields and then rebury them with their heads pointing toward his home to amplify his magical powers. Ahmad thought this ritual would give him great power because he claimed his father's ghost came to him in a dream and commanded him to kill 70 women and drink their saliva.

A comprehensive police search of Ahmad's home property yielded the belongings of 25 different women, even though, at this point, Ahmad had only confessed to killing 16 women. When police searched the sugarcane plantation, they found several more victims buried up to their waist.

The evidence against Ahmad was substantial, and he altered his initial statement. He confessed to the police that he had killed 42 women over eleven years.

Ahmad's three wives, all sisters, were also initially arrested for aiding him in the murders and concealing the corpses. Ahmad had several accomplices, including other family members, who aided him in moving the bodies. One wife led the police to the victims' bodies during the investigation and confessed to her role in the killings. Another wife stated that Ahmad had threatened to kill her if she refused to assist him. Eventually, only one wife, Tumini, remained under arrest; the other two wives were released and left the village.

Over time, the police were able to use forensic evidence, including DNA analysis, dental records, and physical characteristics, to identify victims and establish their cause of death. After the initial bodies were recovered, 80 families came forward with reports of missing family members. The police realized that the actual count of victims could be considerably higher, and more victims may be unearthed.

During their trials, both Ahmad and his wife Tumini

denied the murders, asserting they confessed due to unbearable interrogation torture. Nevertheless, an Indonesian court in North Sumatra found Ahmad guilty and sentenced him to death by firing squad. Tumini also received a death sentence for her role in the killings, although this was later changed to life in prison.

Ahmad's crimes were shocking in their scale and execution. The fact that these horrific acts were carried out with the knowledge and assistance of family members only adds to the chilling nature of the murders. His use of a sugarcane plantation as a burial site and the strangulation of his trusting, immobile victims adds a horrifying twist to these crimes. Ahmad's rituals were grotesque and disturbing, and confidence in his own supernatural prowess empowered him to carry out these killings for an extended period.

"He pretended to be a shaman who could heal any kind of disease. If someone asked to be healed, both their possessions and their lives were taken."

ATTORNEY GENERAL B. NAINGGOLAN

On July 11th, 2008, Ahmad Suradji, then 57, was executed by firing squad. His last request was to see his wife, which was granted.

WARLOCK WANNABE

In 1995, in the town of La Ronge, Saskatchewan, Canada, summer was just getting started. La Ronge is a town situated on the banks of Lac La Ronge with a community that is a mix of Cree and Metis people.

On July 8th, 7-year-old Johnathan Thimpsen was reported missing. Family groups and groups organized by the Royal Canadian Mounted Police set out to search for the boy. Three days after their search started, Johnathan's body was found by a small group of searchers in the woods near his grandmother's house. The child had been murdered in such a gruesome way that the RCMP requested a blackout of information, and the community and the media were kept in the dark. However, news started to leak, and the talk around the small town of La Ronge was of a Satanic cult killing.

Johnathan Thimpsen was born on December 30th, 1987.

As a child, he was known for his playful nature and smile. He was described as outgoing and cheerful by those who knew him. According to his mother, Cindy, his favorite movie was The Lion King, and he loved the character Zorro, the masked hero who used his sword to fight villains.

THE MURDER

Fourteen-year-old Sandy Charles had been hearing voices. They started when his father, Stanley Charles, was killed by a drunk driver. His mother, Jean, noticed how withdrawn her son had become, and she assumed he was just depressed because of his father's death. The voices that Charles called spirits talked him out of killing himself when his father died, but they said other things, too. They talk to him about killing someone else instead. Charles had taken a recent interest in horror movies and occult items like the Ouija board. He'd become obsessed with one horror film he had watched over a dozen times. In the movie *Warlock*, a sorcerer needed the fat from an unbaptized male child to make a flying potion. Charles decided to try the potion himself, but he needed a child as a sacrifice.

For more than a week, Charles planned to murder a boy. He finally settled on Johnathan Thimpsen as his victim. He had a young accomplice, William Martin, only eight years old, who agreed to help the older boy kill

Johnathan. To lure Johnathan away from others, Charles asked him if he wanted to play a game of baseball. Happy to play with Charles and Martin, Johnathan went along with the other boys to look for a ball.

Charles tried to snap Johnathan's neck once the boys were deep into the bushes and not easily seen. When that didn't work, Charles pulled out a paring knife he'd taken from his mother's kitchen and stabbed Johnathan several times in the head and neck, stopping only when the blade wouldn't come out of the boy's eye socket. Johnathan fell to the ground but was still alive, so Charles hit him with a beer bottle that Martin handed him. Finally, Charles put his hand over Johnathan's nose and mouth and suffocated him. The boys had blood on them and returned to Charles' house to clean up and get the items they needed to complete the ritual.

They returned to the body and cut a dozen strips of fat from different places on Johnathan's body. They took it home and boiled the pieces into liquid fat, which Charles poured into a soup can and hid in his basement.

THE INVESTIGATION

During the RCMP investigation, Sandy Charles became a suspect when a witness told police she'd seen all three boys together on the day Johnathan disappeared. Under Canadian law, specifically the Young Offenders Act,

William Martin was too young to be charged with a crime. He was placed in the care of Social Services.

Charles was arrested and confessed. He immediately told police that a spirit in his bedroom told him to kill someone.

During his trial, his attorney portrayed him as suffering from a mental disorder, allowing him to be influenced by the movie and other occult ideas. The psychiatrists who examined him supported this, saying Charles was delusional when he committed the murder.

The prosecution's focus was on premeditation. They made the point that Charles could distinguish right from wrong because he and his accomplice had decided to kill a child 10 days before the murder occurred, and they had specifically chosen Thimpsen as their victim.

Charles was found not guilty due to insanity. He was committed to a maximum-security psychiatric hospital. Charles' life in custody has been marked by a series of transfers between psychiatric institutions due to his behavior and his own requests for relocation.

In 1998, Charles escaped custody. The police put out an alert to the surrounding public that Charles was psychotic and dangerous and they should be wary.

> "Sandy Charles was out for an escorted walk and he ran away from his guards. I won't pull any punches. He definitely shouldn't be out there."

CORPORAL BOB BAZIN, RCMP

Thanks to a member of the public who saw him, Charles was captured several kilometers from the psychiatric hospital.

At one point, Charles was transferred to Saskatchewan Hospital, but he started fighting and knocked a nurse unconscious, leading to his return to the Regional Psychiatric Centre. Charles started the fight on purpose because he wanted to leave the Saskatchewan Hospital.

Charles says he's working on his anger issues and has made attempts to socialize with other inmates. He expressed his wishes to eventually be transferred back to Saskatchewan Hospital and be released from care. Now 39, he is still in psychiatric care, and there are no plans to release him.

Michelle Harding is the elected area director for the Metis Nation of Saskatchewan, representing people of mixed white-Indian ancestry, which covers a large portion of the La Ronge community. She discussed in an interview how parental alcoholism, child abandonment, domestic violence, and more exist as ongoing unsolved problems in the native community. She said, "We've not only lost Johnathan, but we've lost another child, and possibly a third, and I think sadly about what their lives could have been like, and also I think what could force an innocent child, or should be innocent at 14, to do something so heinous."

THE CAMPUS CHURCH MURDER

Arlis Kay Perry, born in 1955, tragically met her end on the 12th of October in 1974. At just 19 years old, this American newlywed's life was cut short in a chilling ritualistic murder inside the Stanford Memorial Church, located within the grounds of Stanford University in California. This gruesome event remained an unsolved mystery for over four decades.

Arlis had a normal upbringing in Bismarck, North Dakota, where she met her high-school sweetheart, Bruce Perry. Their school relationship led them to the altar shortly after graduation, marking the beginning of a new chapter in their lives.

In August 1974, the couple moved to the Stanford University campus. Bruce was pursuing his sophomore year in a pre-med program, and Arlis worked as a receptionist at a local law firm. This period should have been one of joy and excitement for the newlyweds as they navigated through the early stages of their married life. However, the tragic event in October would change everything.

THE MURDER

The night of October 12th, 1974, started with a trivial argument between Arlis and Bruce Perry about their car's tire pressure. After the disagreement, Arlis expressed a desire to pray alone in the Stanford Memorial Church, while Bruce chose to go out with friends for the evening. Bruce came home, fell asleep, and awoke before dawn, realizing Arlis had not returned home. He immediately reported her as missing to the Stanford police.

Police officers from the Santa Clara County Sheriff's Office went to the church and reported that all of the church's doors were securely locked. A few hours later, campus security unlocked the church and made a horrifying discovery. Arlis's body was found near the altar in the east transept of the church.

The scene was horrifying. Arlis was found face-up, her hands folded across her chest, with an ice pick sticking out of the back of her head, its handle broken off and missing. Signs of strangulation were evident, and she was naked from the waist down. Two altar candles were found in disturbing positions – one inserted in her vagina and the other between her breasts. Her jeans had been arranged across her legs in a diamond pattern, adding a chilling detail to the seemingly ritual murder.

On the morning of October 13th. The campus security guard who found Arlis was Stephen Crawford, a former Stanford police officer. In the immediate aftermath of the discovery, Crawford provided an account of the events leading up to the gruesome discovery. He claimed to have locked up the church a little after midnight, noticing no apparent activity inside. Crawford said that he rechecked the doors around 2 am and they were still locked. At 5:45 am, while visiting the church to open it for the day, Crawford stated that he found the west side door open, and it appeared to have been forced from the inside.

THE INVESTIGATION

Investigators found semen on a kneeling pillow near Perry's body, a partial palm print on one of the candles, and DNA on Arliss' jeans. The evidence was puzzling, as neither the semen nor the print matched Arliss' husband, Bruce, or Stephen Crawford. The Santa Clara County Sheriff's Office also ruled out any links between the murder and three previous killings in the area dating back to February 1973, later attributed to serial killer John Getreu.

The police initially named Bruce Perry a suspect, but he was ruled out when he passed a police polygraph test. At least seven people were known to be in the Stanford Memorial Church during the night of October 12th and the morning of October 13th. Among them were Arliss and Stephen Crawford. Four other people were identified, but a seventh individual, described as a young man with sandy-colored hair, medium build, and about five-foot-ten, was not identified. A passerby noted that this young man was about to enter the church around midnight, adding another layer of mystery to the case.

In an unexpected turn of events, serial killer David Berkowitz, known as the *Son of Sam*, mentioned the Perry murder in several letters. He suggested that he had heard details of the crime from an alleged culprit called "Manson II." The murder of Arlis Perry happened just five years after the Manson murders. This claim led investigators to interview Berkowitz in prison. However, they concluded Berkowitz had nothing to offer them to move the case forward.

The perplexing circumstances and lack of conclusive evidence led to the case remaining open for years. The Santa Clara County District Attorney's and Sheriff's Office routinely reviewed it as a cold case, hoping for a breakthrough that could provide closure to Arlin's family.

The breakthrough finally came in 2018 when the authorities revisited the cold case. They sent the DNA evidence collected from the jeans at the crime scene for reanalysis, leveraging decades of advancements in DNA technology. This move paid off, and they received a conclusive match this time. The DNA belonged to Stephen Crawford, the same campus security guard who discovered the body in 1974.

Now aged 72, Crawford was the prime suspect. On June 28th, 2018, law enforcement officials arrived at his residence at Camden Avenue in San Jose, California, about 20 miles from Stanford University, to make an arrest. Crawford, perhaps aware of the damning evidence against him, locked his door and committed suicide with a pistol before he could be arrested.

The ritualistic nature of Perry's murder raised questions about whether Crawford could have acted alone. Crawford was a criminal with a rap sheet for stealing several items from Stanford's library. Despite his criminal past, the leap to a satanic ritualistic murder seemed like a significant escalation. Investigators discovered literature on serial killers in Crawford's home, which led them to consider whether Crawford might have been responsible for multiple murders.

Ultimately, the questions of whether Crawford was a serial killer and why he arranged Perry's body ritualistically remain unanswered. Any secrets or motives behind his actions died with him.

THE PROPHET

Jeffrey Lundgren was an American cult leader who identified as a prophet. He led a cult he created rooted in the
Latter Day Saints movement. Lundgren used a unique
method of scripture interpretation that he termed
chiastic, based on identifying repetitive patterns within
text.

Born in 1950 in Independence, Missouri, Lundgren was
raised as a member of the Reorganized Church of Jesus
Christ of Latter Day Saints (RLDS). During his childhood, Lundgren faced severe abuse, particularly from his
father. His teenage years saw him develop expertise in
hunting, a skill he honed while spending time with his
father, leading to his familiarity with firearms.

After high school, Lundgren started Central Missouri
State University. While attending school, he lived in a
house for RLDS youth. This environment allowed him
to meet Alice Keeler. Alice, who had also faced abuse

from her own father, found solace in her bond with Lundgren, and their relationship quickly turned into marriage in 1970. The couple had a son in 1970, and Alice was pregnant again soon after. In total, the couple had four children together.

Lundgren served in the US Navy, stationed in California, but before he could complete his initial term of duty, he asked for an early discharge. He claimed that his family's sustenance hinged on his presence. The military initially denied his request, but Lundgren persevered until the honorable discharge was granted, mere days before his four-year enlistment would have ended anyway.

MOVE TO OHIO

The family struggled financially when he was released from the military. They lived in Missouri with family and finally relocated to Kirtland, Ohio, in 1984. Here, Jeffrey secured employment with the RLDS church. While residing in a church-owned property, he volunteered as a tour guide at the neighboring historic Kirtland Temple, owned by the RLDS Church.

SCRIPTURE INTERPRETATION

As a tour guide, he introduced his teaching of *dividing the word*, also known as *chiastic interpretation,* as a method of scripture interpretation. He claimed to be the originator of this method, which claims all creations of God exhibit mirrored symmetry and scripture should be interpreted using a similar approach. He used the Kirtland Temple as an example, noting its right side mirrored its left.

Lundgren proposed that the middle sentence of a series of scripture sentences represented *truth* if the preceding and following sentences were consistent. If there was a contradiction between the sentences before and after, he deemed the middle sentence false. Lundgren claimed that his relocation to Ohio was influenced by the word *Ohio* exhibiting *chiastic* properties. His unique approach to scriptural interpretation attracted many followers, and as a tour guide, he had daily opportunities to gather more. The church mandated that all offerings from temple visitors be given to the church. Lundgren kept some contributions for himself. His employment as a guide had no salary, only housing, and Lundgren was fired three years later when he was implicated for theft from the church.

After his dismissal, Lundgren and his family moved from their church-provided accommodation to a nearby farmhouse. Gradually, he began urging his followers to liquidate their possessions and use their credit cards to buy provisions and join him. He insisted they address him as *Dad* and refer to his wife Alice as *Mom*. Several followers began to establish residence within his new household. These included Kevin Currie, Richard Brand, Greg Winship, Sharon Bluntschly, Daniel Kraft, and Debbie Olivarez. However, Ronald and Susan Luff,

Dennis and Tonya Patrick, and Dennis and Cheryl Avery chose to maintain independent living arrangements.

TEACHINGS CHANGE

The RLDS church officially excommunicated Lundgren. Following this formal expulsion, Lundgren's leadership took an oppressive turn. He sought to seclude his followers from external influence, fostering an environment of complete dependency on him. In his new location, Lundgren continued his teachings but changed the focus of his sermons to the RLDS Kirtland Temple. He told his disciples they were compelled to reclaim this temple, which would then be lifted by an earthquake. At this point, he said Christ would return and establish Zion. Lundgren initially selected May 3rd, 1988, coinciding with his own birthday, as the day to retake the temple. As the date got closer, he postponed the plan, judging that the time was not right. Lundgren shared his communications with God and his visions.

Lundgren started focusing his prayer meetings on the Book of Revelations and the Book of Mormon. Over time, his fanaticism intensified. Regular discussions of apocalyptic scenarios and violent tactics became a common occurrence. Lundgren attempted to create discord among his followers, and he encouraged them to report each other's behavior. This told him who to trust.

MURDER PLANNING

In his prayer meetings, he also spoke about "tending to the vineyard" and how it would be necessary to eliminate 10 of his followers before Zion could be actualized. In anticipation of the assault on the Kirtland temple, the group's male members underwent paramilitary training. The Averys, who were only loosely associated with the group, were extended invitations to just a handful of Lundgren's prayer gatherings and none of the military-style training.

Lundgren began to employ practices of mind control. He enforced a restriction on communication among his cult members. Cult members gathering and speaking amongst themselves was called *murmuring* by Lundgren, and he deemed it a sin. He would secretly listen in on any conversations of cult members and then confront them with the knowledge explaining that he had a mind-reading ability. He attempted to persuade his followers that he was the final prophet of God.

Some of his followers were more devout than others. His attention returned to the Avery family, who were mostly noncompliant with his imposed regulations and had refused to move into his house. Lundgren perceived Avery as weak and began disparaging him once his usefulness waned. Despite being one of its most substantial financiers, Avery was frequently blamed for the sect's difficulties. Dennis Avery had established a modest bank account for his family's needs and didn't want to give the money to Lundgren, who viewed this decision as sinful.

THE MURDERS

The Avery family was invited to the farmhouse under the pretense of a group gathering and dinner. They had no idea that days earlier, Lundgren had instructed his most obedient followers to dig a pit in the barn. Those followers were also aware of who would be going in the hole.

Under Jeffrey Lundgren's directive, on April 10th, 1989, two devoted followers murdered the Avery family. From oldest to youngest, each Avery was led out to the barn, bound, and thrown into the pit. Dennis Avery and his wife, Cheryl, were shot multiple times while lying bound in the hole. Their children were not spared. Trina, age 15, Rebecca, and Karen, ages 13 and seven, were also shot and killed after being thrown in the pit with their deceased parents. After the shootings, the dirt and rocks were dumped back into the hole. After the murders, Lundgren held a prayer meeting.

RELOCATION

Following the murders, Lundgren relocated from Ohio to Davis, West Virginia, with his remaining followers living in tents. The men continued their military-style training with firearms, and some members of the cult went into the community and got jobs. During his time in West Virginia, Lundgren selected Tonya Patrick to be his second wife. The arrangement didn't go well, so he chose Kathryn Johnson to fulfill that role. This decision upset Kathryn's husband, Larry Johnson, and stirred unrest in the group. By October 1989, Lundgren, his family, and ten followers left West Virginia and relocated to Missouri.

In December 1989, Larry Johnson contacted law enforcement to report the Avery family murders. He took them to the now-deserted Lundgren farm in Ohio, where the remains of the Avery family were exhumed from the pit. This revelation caused intense media coverage and triggered a nationwide manhunt for Lundgren and his associates. The search intensified with the FBI's involvement, leading to the eventual capture of 13 members of Lundgren's sect in early 1990. This group included both Lundgren and his wife and one of his sons.

Lundgren was tried, found guilty of the murders, and sentenced to death. His wife, Alice, received five life sentences for her involvement in conspiracy, complicity, and kidnapping. Their son, Damon, was sentenced to a life term of 120 years. Luff, who was heavily involved in planning and carrying out the murders with Lundgren, was given a sentence of 170 years to life. Daniel Kraft received a sentence of 50 years to life. Five other cult members were released in 2010 or early 2011, according to their original plea agreements.

By August 2006, Lundgren had exhausted all avenues for appeal. In a last attempt to delay the inevitable, on October 17th, 2006, Judge Gregory L. Frost issued a provisional order postponing Lundgren's execution. Lundgren tried to join a lawsuit alongside five other Ohio death row inmates. His argument claimed that his obesity would create disproportionate pain during the application of the lethal injection., He said this constituted cruel and unusual punishment.

The state's Attorney General, Jim Petro, challenged this stance, appealing to the United States Court of Appeals for the Sixth Circuit in Cincinnati. That court issued an order permitting the execution to proceed. The U.S. Supreme Court declined a last-minute plea to halt Lundgren's execution, and Governor Bob Taft denied any clemency request.

Lundgren was executed on October 24th, 2006. No one claimed his body, so he was buried in the Southern Ohio Correctional Facility's cemetery.

FRIEND IN THE PARK

In a London court in February 2001, Angeles Villar-Fernandez and her relatives stood up and threw a water jug, a court folder with papers, and anything else they could reach at 52-year-old Edward Crowley from Teesside. They screamed at him and cried until they were removed from the courtroom. Angeles, the mother of murdered 12-year-old Diego Piniero-Villar, was distraught after listening to the testimony of Crowley, the confessed devil worshiper who killed her son, Diego.

On May 10th, 2000, three days after Diego was murdered, Angeles said to the newspaper The Mirror:

"I can't believe my angel is dead. My son can never be replaced in my heart. I can't believe he has gone. I feel he is still here walking around.

We were alone for six years after I divorced Diego's father until I met my present husband. Maybe I loved him too much because he was the centre of my world. Some people said I over-protected him, but clearly, I didn't protect him enough. Diego, he didn't believe there was evil in the world. Every day, I used to tell him not to speak to strangers.

I have no faith in justice now. I am never going to feel peace. I have been condemned to death in life like a robot. I feel like I have been killed. I can't see a way forward without Diego."

TWO YEARS EARLIER

Diego Piniero-Villar, a boy in the Spanish community in London's Covent Garden area, met Edward Crowley, a drifter more than four times his age, in a park in central London. The other kids in the park threw rocks at the man, and Diego chose to be kind and speak to him. Unaware of the danger, the innocent boy befriended the scruffy stranger, a decision that would ultimately cost him his life.

Diego didn't know that Crowley had a long history of mental illness and was obsessed with the occult. Crowley's fascination with the occult dated back to 1998 when he changed his name from Henry Allen Bibby to Edward Alexander Crowley to honor Aleister Crowley, an infamous self-proclaimed black arts magician.

The relationship between Diego and Crowley began with frequent conversations near the swings of the dilapidated playground. These interactions gradually evolved into trips to a local arcade and visits to a local public pool. Crowley bought Diego small gifts and food, and Diego, who thought the man was his friend, enjoyed spending time with him.

Diego kept his friendship with Crowley a secret for a while, and it's unclear whether this was Diego's choice or something Crowley insisted on. Still, during the Summer of 1999, Diego's mother realized that her son had an unusual friendship with an older man. She contacted the police, and they asked Diego about his friend. While there was no evidence of child sex abuse, the relationship was deemed uncomfortably physical. Crowley and Diego would have play fights, during which Crowley would lick Diego's ear and tickle him. During their investigation, police found witnesses that said Crowley routinely approached other children in the park. The reports led to increased police scrutiny of Crowley, but they didn't question him.

In the Fall of 1999, Crowley himself visited the Holborn police station. He confessed to having a relationship with a 12-year-old boy, which he described as "loving but not primarily sexual." Crowley retracted this claim as quickly as he made it. A psychiatric nurse working with police reviewed the case and concluded that Crowley was a risk to young boys.

Diego's mother started receiving phone calls from an anonymous man asking for her son and started to worry even more for his safety. It was clear to her that Diego was caught in a dangerous and inappropriate relationship. At this point, Diego had grown uncomfortable with Crowley's attentions and started avoiding him.

THE MESSAGES

Police made a chilling discovery at the park. Scrawled onto the seats of the old swings were two messages presumably written by Crowley and left as personal notes to Diego. One message read: "I will always love you, Diego. Please forgive me for everything. I couldn't stand the pain. One day you'll know how much you hurt me. How much I need you."

The second message said, "Always cheat others before they cheat you - if they are clever enough. I wasn't, and I wouldn't want to be. Bravo, mi chico Latino," a Spanish phrase translating to *Bravo, my Latin boy*. Based on the messages, Crowley was arrested on November 3rd under the suspicion of indecently assaulting Diego, but the police had no concrete evidence, and he was quickly released.

One month later, Crowley visited the school Diego attended in West London. He painted a message in Spanish and English across three doors, "Why did you cheat me Diego? Why all the lies? I should hate you, but I don't. Alex."

Crowley was arrested outside the school and caught in the act of vandalism. He appeared before Marylebone magistrates the following day, pleading guilty to causing criminal damage. Despite the increasing severity of his actions, he was given a two-year conditional discharge and released back onto the streets.

Police provided Diego with a police-issued mobile phone, enabling him to dial emergency services instantly. Patrols around the school were stepped up, and his stepfather, Juan Fernandez, began escorting him throughout West London.

Several days later, Crowley was charged with harassment, arrested, and sent for a mental health assessment. The psychiatrist who saw Crowley in prison said he was dangerous and should stay in prison.

THE FAILURE

Despite the escalating threats and concerns regarding Crowley's mental health, the criminal justice system experienced significant failures. On March 20th, after three months in custody, the prosecutor admitted that Crowley's case was not ready to go to the Crown Court for trial. Ignoring objections from the police, a district judge granted Crowley bail with strict conditions.

Crowley was ordered not to contact Diego, go near the boy's home or school, or visit the park. He was also required to report daily to a police station, although this condition was relaxed after two weeks.

At some point, Crowley stopped reporting to police, and they had no idea where he was. He had no monitoring by social services and was off any medication that had been prescribed when he was incarcerated.

In the months during his captivity, Crowley developed a grudge and decided to take revenge. On the evening of May 7th, Diego's stepfather, Juan Fernandez, asked Diego and his stepbrother Roberto, 15, to run an errand. As they passed the park, the place where Diego had first met Crowley, he was waiting for them.

Armed with a kitchen knife, he stabbed the older boy, Roberto. He then turned on Diego. Despite his fear, Diego managed to dial 999 on his police-provided mobile phone. The operator on the other end heard desperate screams as Crowley brutally stabbed Diego more than 20 times.

By the time the ambulance arrived, it was too late. Diego Piniero-Villar was pronounced dead upon arrival at St. Thomas's Hospital. Roberto survived his wounds.

Police now had a murder investigation, although their prime suspect, Crowley, was arrested immediately. They discovered that Crowley was born in Middlesbrough,

England, in 1948 and had spent most of his life jobless and drifting. His medical records revealed a history of attempted suicides and at least seven instances of drug overdoses.

When Crowley was arrested after the murder, police found a piece of paper in his bag. It was covered in references to child sacrifice in religion, black magic, and classical myth. At the top of the page were the Latin words "Delendus est D. Piniero" which translates to *D. Piniero must be destroyed*.

After his trial, Crowley was sentenced to life in prison.

After the trial, Diego's mother told the media, "I wanted to kill him myself when I saw him in court. I feel the law is not good enough for child murder. It should be the death penalty for this man."

THE WITCH'S CAULDRON

The serial killer Leonarda Cianciulli, also known as the *soapmaker of Correggio*, was born in 1894 in Montella, Italy. She died in 1970 at the age of 76.

Leonarda's early life was marred with challenges and hardship. Born to a mother who was forced to marry her rapist, Leonarda was not loved by her parents. Her mother told her as she was growing up that she was cursed. Leonarda attempted to commit suicide twice at a young age as a result of her tormented childhood.

Defying her mother's wishes, she chose her spouse, marrying an office clerk in 1914. It was a brave step to gain control over her own life and escape the arranged marriage planned by her mother. The couple moved to Irpinia in Southern Italy. Leonarda and her husband had 17 pregnancies, but unfortunately, only four children lived past the age of ten.

When a traveling fortune teller warned Leonarda that all of her children would die, she changed. Leonarda became a fiercely protective mother to her four surviving children.

An earthquake destroyed her home in the 1930s, but she persevered and opened her own shop in town to make more money for the family. She was well-liked in her community.

Leonarda was also deeply superstitious. In the town where she lived, people still practiced several pagan rituals. She felt these rituals would keep her children safe, so she kept up the tradition. Still haunted by her mother's claim that she was cursed and also by the fortune teller's prophecy, she pulled several of her own teeth and burned them in a special ritual. She decided the basic pagan customs for good fortune were not enough, and she soon turned to darker rituals to protect her remaining children. Her favorite son, Giuseppe, had recently signed up to join the Italian Army, and he needed her protection even more. Between 1939 and 1940, Leonarda, then in her mid-40s, murdered three women, believing she needed to make human sacrifices to achieve her goals.

FAUSTINA SETTI

Her first victim, Faustina Setti, was a spinster. She had asked Leonarda to help her find a husband. Leonarda told Setti about an eligible man located in the distant town of Pola. She made Setti promise to tell no one that she was helping her. The manipulation didn't end there. She cleverly convinced Setti to write numerous letters and postcards intended for her family and friends. The letters reassured her loved ones that she had gone to Pola and that all was going well.

On the day of her journey to Pola, Setti made a final visit to Leonarda's home. To celebrate the matchmaking, Leonarda offered Setti a glass of wine. She told her it was a special wine, but prior to the visit, Leonarda had laced the wine with a powerful sedative. Once the drug took effect, Leonarda used an axe and murdered Setti. She calmly dragged the lifeless body into a hidden closet. The macabre scene continued as she dismembered Setti's body into nine segments, carefully collecting the blood from each limb into a waiting basin.

Leonardo's memoir detailed how she used Setti's body to make soap and tea cakes.

"I threw the pieces into a pot, added seven kilos of caustic soda, which I had bought to make soap, and stirred the whole mixture until the pieces dissolved in a thick, dark mush that I poured into several buckets and emptied in a nearby septic tank. As for the blood in the basin, I waited until it had coagulated, dried it in the oven, ground it and mixed it with flour, sugar, chocolate, milk and eggs, as well as a bit of margarine, kneading all the ingredients together. I made lots of crunchy tea cakes and served them to the ladies who came to visit, though Giuseppe and I also ate them."

Leonarda Cianciulli

AN EMBITTERED SOUL'S CONFESSIONS

FRANCESCA SOAVI

The next victim was Francesca Soavi. Leonarda had deceitfully promised her employment at a girls' school in Piacenza. Like Setti, Soavi was persuaded to draft post-cards to her friends outlining her new journey to a new life and job. When Soavi visited Leonarda before leaving, she was offered the drugged wine and then killed with an axe. The dreadful act took place on September 5th, 1940. Soavi's body was disposed of in the same manner as Setti's.

VIRGINIA CACIOPPO

A few weeks later, Virginia Cacioppo, a one-time opera singer, was the final victim of Leonarda. For Cacioppo, Leonarda fabricated a job opportunity as a secretary for an impresario based in Florence. Cacioppo was similarly advised to keep her destination secret, and she agreed. She visited Leonarda for the last time on September 30th, 1940, and her murder followed the same ritual as the previous two. Leonarda wrote about this in her memoir.

"The fate of this victim was no different from the others... Her flesh was plump and white. After it had dissolved, I mixed in a bottle of cologne, and after a lengthy period of boiling, I was able to produce a decently creamy soap. I distributed soap bars to my neighbors and friends. The baked goods were also improved — that woman was indeed sweet."

The cakes she baked with her gruesome ingredients were served to her unsuspecting neighbors and her sons.

Leonarda's crimes came to light after Cacioppo disappeared. Cacioppo's sister-in-law told police that Leonarda was the last person who saw Cacioppo alive. The police started looking at Leonarda's son Giuseppe and accused him of Cacioppo's disappearance. Faced with accusations against her beloved son, Leonarda confessed to everything — the killings, the soap, the cakes, and the chilling rituals behind them.

While awaiting trial, Leonarda wrote her memoir, *An*

Embittered Soul's Confessions, chronicling her life and crimes. In it, she gave recipes for some of her dishes that included human remains.

"I used to mix human blood with chocolate and add an exquisite flavor made of tangerine, aniseed, vanilla, and cinnamon. Sometimes I added a sprinkling of powder from human bones…I plunged in a ladle and picked out a substance of soapy appearance. As a matter of fact, the flesh had been converted into a sort of wax, in which I fixed a wick. It made a perfect candle, which I lighted. Greatness of God, what a superb flame!"

Leonarda's trial lasted three days, leading to a sentence of 30 years in prison and three years in an asylum. Leonarda died in the asylum in October 1970 from a stroke.

Today, you can see Leonarda Cianciulli's axe and the pot she used to boil her victims' bodies at the Criminology Museum in Rome.

CHANGING FAITH

MARCH 5TH 1986

Upon being awakened by the gunshot that killed her husband, Lee Bellofatto, Vonda was promptly shot in the face by her own son. To avoid immediate suspicion, her son, Sean Sellers, attempted to stage the crime scene to make it appear as if an intruder had committed the murders. In a moment of pre-planning, he made sure he wore only his underwear during the murders to limit the amount of blood spatter on his clothing. Sellers was 17, and his mother's murder was his third in less than two years.

Court statement by Sean Sellers:

"My life stunk. I was angry with my parents. I continually thought about suicide. I just wanted out. I sat there in my pickup, wishing I had either the guts to blow my

brains out or a way to find a new world and leave everything behind. I had been up for three days. I was out of
speed. Tonight, I would get some sleep. I drove home,
did some homework, performed a ritual, and slept. My
next clear memory is a jail cell two days later. I had taken
my father's .44 revolver and shot both my parents in the
head as they slept. In a year, the memories of that night
would haunt me. I had stood in front of my mother's
convulsing body, watching blood pour from a hole in
her face, and laughed a hideous giggle. I had felt relieved
as if the world's oppression had been lifted from my
shoulders. But for now, all knew was that my life was
destroyed. I had given Satan everything, and now I sat in
a jail cell without a family. I no longer wanted to be a
Satanist."

In a later confession, Sellers admitted his involvement in
another act of violence before the murder of his mother
and stepfather. In 1985, Sellers murdered Robert Paul
Bower, a 32-year-old convenience store clerk at Circle K
who had refused to sell his friend beer.

Court statement by Sean Sellers:

"It was time to prove our allegiance to Satan. We
began breaking the Ten Commandments. Only
one remained, "Thou shall not murder." We talked
about things such as waiting at a stop sign in the
middle of nowhere and blowing away the first
person who was fool enough to obey the law. We

talked about torture for a friend's ex-girlfriend. We would tie her down, slice her breasts, cut her throat, but only after we would rape her for a few days. It was after a lust ritual with my second priest that Satan took over our actions. In a game-like surreal euphoria, we drove to a convenience store where a man worked who had insulted my friend's girlfriend and refused to sell him beer. In my hand I held a cold steel killing tool a .357 magnum loaded with hollow points. After much conversation with the man who thought we were friends, my friend distracted him and I raised the gun from beneath the counter, pointed it at his head, and squeezed the trigger. It missed. I fired again. My friend cut him off from getting away. The second shot had only injured him. I caught him. His terror-stricken eyes searched mine for mercy behind the smoking barrel. I squeezed the trigger and he collapsed, knocked back from the impact— dead. Blood covered The rear wall and ran onto the floor. And two teenagers walked out, taking no money, no merchandise. Only the life of an innocent man for Satan."

Sean Richard Sellers was born on May 18th, 1969, and executed on February 4th, 1999, at the age of 29. The killing of Bower, along with the murders of his mother and stepfather, solidified Sellers' place as a convicted triple murderer. He remains the only person executed for a crime perpetrated before the age of seventeen.

In addition to his young age at the time of his crimes, Sellers's case attracted worldwide attention due to other parts of his personal story. Sellers claimed that he was a practicing Satanist at the time of his crimes. This shocking assertion was only the beginning of his attempt to explain his violent acts. He said he was under the influence of a demonic entity named *Ezurate* when he committed the murders, and this possession meant he should not be held responsible for the murders. Sellers reported that he had read *The Satanic Bible* by Anton LaVey hundreds of times between the ages of 15 and 16. When his case went to trial, his defense team claimed that Sellers was addicted to the game *Dungeons & Dragons,* but Sellers contradicted this in his own trial testimony, stating that the game had no part in his crimes.

Despite these defenses, the jury was not swayed. Sellers was found guilty of three homicides and sentenced to death in 1986. At the time, Oklahoma law did not provide the option for a life sentence without the possibility of parole. This option was introduced a year later. One juror later stated that the jury feared Sellers would be paroled in 7 to 15 years, a term they felt was insufficient for his crimes. Consequently, they opted for the death penalty.

JAILHOUSE CONVERSION

Sellers converted to Christianity in prison, a transformation he publicized and used as part of his bid for clemency. He again claimed he was innocent of his crimes because he was under demonic possession at the time of the murders.

His friends started a website on his behalf, which served as a platform for his campaign. His religious conversion, his age at the time of his crimes, and his previous involvement in Satanism were highlighted as reasons for reconsideration of his sentence. While incarcerated, he authored a book of love stories and poems titled *Shuladore*. The book was self-published and sold via his website.

LIFE IN PRISON

Sellers made numerous videos from prison. His story was featured on *The Oprah Winfrey Show* and *Geraldo*, where he discussed his prior involvement with Satanism. His crimes were included in documentaries about Satanism and serial killers. His personal life also saw significant changes during this time. Sellers got married in prison on February 14th, 1995. The marriage was short-lived and was annulled in 1997.

Despite Sellers' public declarations of faith, his sincerity was met with skepticism by some of his step-siblings.

They doubted the authenticity of his conversion. Among his family, only his step-grandfather believed he was being genuine. The prison chaplain believed in Sellers' earnest conversion.

Sellers' conviction and sentence marked the beginning of a series of legal battles. In 1999, during his appeal to the 10th U.S. Circuit Court of Appeals, Sellers claimed that at the time of the murders, he suffered from a multiple personality disorder, now known as dissociative identity disorder. Sellers was interviewed by Dr. Dorothy Lewis, a recognized professor in the field of psychiatry. Lewis diagnosed Sellers with chronic psychosis, paranoid schizophrenia, and significant mood disorders. Six years post-trial, in 1992, Sellers was diagnosed with Multiple Personality Disorder (MPD) by a panel of three mental health professionals. This condition is characterized by the presence of distinct or alternative personalities within the individual. Two of the evaluating physicians independently interacted with two of Sellers' alternative personalities. One was named *The Controller,* and the other was called *Danny.* Danny exhibited left-handedness despite Sellers being right-handed.

Some psychiatric experts dismissed Sellers' claims of mental illness. These experts argued that any genuine mental illness would have been diagnosed shortly after Sellers' arrest, not seven years later. Similarly, prison officials cast suspicion on Sellers' claims by asserting they had witnessed him rehearsing evidence of mental illness and receiving coaching from his attorneys. The court ultimately ruled that this issue was raised too late to be considered on appeal.

Sellers brought his insanity claim in front of the clemency board, but it, too, refused to consider the issue. The board was swayed by the prison officials' statements and the lengthy delay in diagnosing the illness. Sellers made further appeals to the U.S. Supreme Court, but the court declined to hear his case.

The impending execution of Sellers provoked condemnation from a wide range of sources, including the European Union, Archbishop Desmond Tutu, the American Bar Association, and Bianca Jagger. Many of these voices raised concerns about his age at the time of the crimes, while others argued that his religious work from prison outweighed the state's need to execute him.

Despite these appeals and condemnations, Sellers was executed by lethal injection on February 4th, 1999, at the Oklahoma State Penitentiary in McAlester, Oklahoma. In his final statement, he addressed his step-siblings and spoke of hatred, healing, and God's presence. In his last moments, Sellers sang modern Christian music and made a final declaration of his readiness to meet his end.

A GAME OF CHESS

On July 27th, 1992, 18-year-old Alexander Pichushkin murdered his friend and fellow student Mikhail Odichuk. The incident occurred in Bitssa Park in Moscow. Mikhail was found dead in the sewer several days later. Alexander originally intended to ask Mikhail to help him kill other people. Mikhail thought he was kidding when he first proposed the idea. Once he realized Alexander wasn't joking, he got up to leave the park. This provoked Alexander, and he hit Mikhail in the head with a hammer. Alexander dragged his body over to the opening of a sewer and dropped him in. Alexander got away with this murder, which was deemed a suicide by police. This would be his first of 48 murders, and he wouldn't be stopped for another 14 years.

Alexander was born in 1974 in Moscow, Russia. He lived in a two-bedroom apartment near Bitssa Park with his mother and brother. During his early years, Alexander was an average child. However, an incident at the age of four changed his behavior. He hit his forehead hard while playing on a swing. Medical experts suggest that this injury might have affected his frontal cortex, a region of the brain associated with impulse control and aggression. After this accident, his behavior at school became increasingly aggressive, and he was transferred to a specialized learning institution. There, he was subjected to physical and verbal maltreatment from peers, exacerbating his aggressive tendencies.

He was stable when his maternal grandfather took care of him. Recognizing Alexander's aptitude, he introduced him to chess. The game provided an outlet for Alexander, with Bitssa Park becoming a regular venue for his chess matches. The death of his grandfather in 1988 meant Alexander had to move back with his family, and his aggressive behavior quickly resurfaced.

TEENAGE YEARS

Following Mikhail's murder, Alexander led a regular life for nearly a decade. He was employed as a shelf stacker at a supermarket, but personal relationships and romantic connections were challenging for him. During these teenage years, his alcohol consumption increased, and slowly, his compulsion to murder again grew, too. By 2001, he had murdered 11 people in Bitssa Park.

THE PARK

Bitssa Park, or Bitsyevskiy Park, is located in the southern region of Moscow. Covering 2,700 acres, it's one of the largest parks in Russia and was popular with the locals. The park's reputation changed when Alexander began to murder within its confines. Parents warned children against venturing into the park unaccompanied, and adults became increasingly vigilant.

Primarily targeting older, often homeless men, Alexander would meet them in the park and offer them alcohol. He'd tell the men that he'd just lost his dog or it was the anniversary of his dog's death, and he wanted to share a drink at the grave with someone. At the earliest opportunity and usually near one of the many sewer entrances, he would hit the victim on the head with a hammer, and they would fall into the sewer, or he would drag their body into it. The intricate sewer system beneath the park made it difficult to discover the crimes immediately.

"I have nightmares ... A dog. It lived with me a long time. She died. It was my fault. I treated it, how to say, not very ... She could have been saved. It was a bad situation ... it left something in my subconscious."

PICHUSHKIN, IN AN INTERVIEW

MARINA VIRICHEVA

Marina Viricheva, one of three survivors, was a 19-year-old expectant mother facing financial difficulties. Alexander offered her inexpensive vodka, and they discussed the possibility of selling stolen goods he had hidden in the park's sewer system. When Viricheva went with him to look at these goods, Alexander pushed her into the sewer. Her clothing caught on the way in and saved her. Motivated by the well-being of her unborn child, Viricheva managed to escape and approach the police. Unfortunately, her status as an undocumented immigrant became a focal point for the police, leading to no action on her complaint of attempted murder.

MURDER METHOD

Alexander usually used a hammer to strike his victims in the head. He would sometimes insert a vodka bottle or twigs and flowers into the resulting wound before putting them in the sewer. He claimed he loved the sound of the skull cracking, and when he killed, he felt like God. He typically approached his victims from behind to minimize the risk to himself and to prevent staining his clothing. Ten of the 49 victims lived near the residential complex where Alexander lived. He has said in police interviews that he aimed to kill 64 people, the number of squares on a chessboard. He had a chessboard that he used to mark each murder, but he later admitted that if he'd gotten to 64, he would have kept killing.

On June 16th, 2006, Alexander was arrested. His last known victim was Marina Moskalyova, aged thirty-six. Before her disappearance, she informed her son about her plan to meet a young man. When she failed to return home, her son called the police. Her remains were eventually located, and police found a metro ticket in her purse. Surveillance footage from the metro station revealed that she met Alexander Pichushkin. Once arrested, Alexander openly confessed to his crimes and assisted law enforcement in locating several victims that hadn't been found. In addition to the chessboard, investigators found a diary that contained the details of his murders.

During his trial, Alexander was housed within a protective glass enclosure, partly to shield him from potential retaliation by bereaved families. In October 2007, he was found guilty of 48 counts of murder and three counts of attempted murder. Alexander requested the court to acknowledge an additional eleven deaths under his name. The judge spent an hour recounting the extensive list of offenses and subsequent judgments. Some speculate he wanted more confirmed kills than serial killer Andrei Chikatilo, *The Butcher of Rostov*, who killed more than 52 people.

Alexander was ultimately sentenced to life in prison, with a directive to spend the first fifteen years in solitary confinement. In contrast to his asking the judge to add more murder victims, Alexander challenged the severity of his sentence, describing it as "overly harsh," and he requested it be reduced to twenty-five years. As of 2017, Alexander resided in the city of Kharp in an Arctic supermax penal colony named *Polar Owl*, where he spends his time in solitary confinement.

"When I was brought to prison, I was not in a good mood. Now it's gotten better, I have completely adapted. They have ideal water here. It's so hot, I even have to dilute it with cold water. For all the time that I have been here, my hair was cut only once. Do you know how much time they give me to take a shower - five whole minutes!"

PICHUSHKIN, IN AN INTERVIEW
WITH RUSSIAN TABLOID, *TVOI
DEN*, 2008

HUNTING

In 1983, in Anchorage, 18-year-old Cindy Paulson was found walking down Sixth Avenue in a terrible state. She was barefoot and had handcuffs on her wrists. A man in a truck saw her running and stopped to rescue her. Later, she was able to give a statement to the local law enforcement about what happened.

Paulson, who sometimes worked as a sex worker, described a man in his thirties who had initially wanted sex in his car but had offered her more money if she came to his house. She wavered but complied in the end. Once she got in his car, he pulled out a gun and handcuffed her. Once at his home, he kept her immobile with a chain around her neck. She said she'd been subjected to many brutal sexual assaults throughout the night. Even though the man told her his name was Don, she could see pictures and hunting trophies in the room that said *Robert Hansen*. He noticed her looking at them and realized she knew his real name.

The next day, the man told her he was going to take her to a secluded cabin in the Matanuska-Susitna Valley, roughly 35 miles away from Anchorage, and that they were going by plane. He said he'd taken seven other women there and would fly her there, "make love" to her once, and have her back in Anchorage the next day by 11 am. She didn't believe him and was sure he would kill her. She knew her only opportunity for escape would come between the house and the airfield.

The next day at 5 am, he loaded Paulson and some supplies into his car. When he arrived at the airfield, he pulled up to his two-seater, Piper Super Cub, got out, and started making his preparations for the flight. Paulson was still handcuffed in the car's back seat, but she threw her body into the front seat and opened the passenger door. She ran. Hansen saw her and gave chase, but she made it through the tree line onto the road.

Thankful that her 5-hour ordeal was over, Paulson asked the driver to take her to the local motel where her boyfriend sometimes stayed.

Robert Hansen walked back to his car on the airfield and sped away. The airfield security officer made note of his departure and wrote down his license plate number.

Cindy Paulson, still in handcuffs, called her boyfriend via the front desk, and the front desk clerk called the Anchorage Police Department.

When the police interviewed Robert Hansen, a resident of Anchorage, he looked just like Paulson had described him. He wore glasses, had a face scarred by acne, and owned the aircraft she described. He even had the stutter that Paulson had mentioned to the police.

ARRESTS

Hansen's rap sheet said he'd spent time in prison in his early twenties for burning down a school bus barn in Pocahontas, Iowa. He'd been married at the time, and his wife left him during his 11-month incarceration. A prison psychiatrist who evaluated him in 1960 diagnosed him with depression and schizophrenic episodes. The doctor noted that Hansen had an *infantile personality* and was obsessed with getting back at people he felt had wronged him. When he moved from Iowa to Alaska with his new wife, he was arrested three times. Once for the abduction and attempted assault of a local woman and again for sexually assaulting another woman. The third time was for shoplifting a chainsaw.

When questioned, Hansen admitted to meeting Paulson, but he insisted she was trying to falsely implicate him over a money dispute. His claims were supported by a solid alibi provided by a friend. Authorities were reluctant to detain him. Hansen, who, despite his previous legal issues, was a local baker, had a family and children and had a positive standing within the community. The police released him.

~

Robert Hansen's early life was challenging. As a child, he was employed in the family bakery for extended periods. Despite his natural left-handedness, his parents forced him to use his right hand, leading to a persistent stutter. As a teenager, he had severe acne, was introverted, and had no lasting friendships or relationships with his teen peers. As a loner, he developed a keen interest in game hunting with a rifle and a bow.

Hansen started stalking and murdering human victims in the early 1970's. His ritual was usually the same. He would invite a woman, usually a sex worker, into his car and sexually assault her at gunpoint. He would then take her to a remote location where he "hunted" her like wild game. This usually culminated in the victim's death by gunshots or stabbings.

Police believe Hansen's inaugural murder victim was 18-year-old Celia van Zanten. Van Zanten was kidnapped on December 22nd, 1971, and froze to death in the wilderness after escaping from her abductor. Her body was found three days later, on Christmas Day. This set the pattern for the murder of 17+ women over the next 12 years.

~

Alaska State Troopers had growing concerns about the existence of a serial killer. Several women, primarily involved in strip club dancing and sex work, had vanished, and several bodies had been discovered.

Sherry Morrow, a 23-year-old dancer, told her friends she was meeting a photographer to do a set of nude photos. She went missing, and hunters found her body in a shallow grave along the banks of the Knik River near Anchorage. She'd been shot in the back with a .223 Ruger Mini-14 hunting rifle while naked and was redressed post-mortem before burial.

When two sets of remains were found in the Matanuska-Susitna Valley, along with .223 caliber shell casings nearby, the suspicions surrounding Hansen heightened. This is where Hansen said he was taking Paulson. However, clear-cut evidence was still elusive.

The troopers asked the FBI for help with a criminal profile. Retired FBI agent John Douglas, recognized for his ground-breaking work in criminal profiling, said their offender was an experienced hunter, suffered from low self-esteem, and had encountered rejection from women. He said the offender would likely take mementos from each kill, and he may have a stutter.

Law enforcement obtained a warrant to search Hansen's plane, vehicle, and residences. Police found an aviation map marked with "Xs." Some of the "Xs corresponded with places where bodies had been found. In the basement of Hansen's primary residence, police found several pieces of women's jewelry, one of which belonged to one of their female victims. When confronted with his evidence, Hansen confessed to sexually assaulting 30 women and murdering 17 of them.

As part of a plea deal, Hansen took police on a six-hour helicopter tour of 17 burial sites located in Southcentral Alaska, 12 of which were previously unknown to law enforcement. He refused to identify all of the marks on his map, and based on evidence that was found, police estimate that he may have killed 37 victims.

Hansen received a prison sentence of 461 years without parole and spent most of his time incarcerated at the Anchorage Correctional Complex in Seward.
He died of natural causes in 2014 at the age of 75.

The media portrayed Hansen as a "sexually frustrated Anchorage baker." In a 1984 interview with the *Daily Sitka Sentinel*, he said, "If you look real close at me, you'll see I used to have a tremendous amount of pimples on my face. I guess it's because I grew up in a bakery. I'm addicted to sweets….My gosh, I looked like a freak and sounded like one. Consequently, I never had many girls that were interested in me."

When asked about taking sex workers to his cabin, he said, "As long as she would go along with what I wanted out there, okay. We'd go home, and that was it." When pressed on what would happen if they didn't go along with his plan, he stuttered and said, "They…They stayed."

FROM KILLER CASE FILES: ROUTE 128 STRANGULATION

"They're wonderful people [The Gravel Family]… a real close-knit family. It's been so tough on them all these years. She's on their mind every day."

FORMER STATE POLICE DETECTIVE
SERGEANT ELAINE GILL

HAMILTON, MASSACHUSETTS

In 2007, Rosemary Diskin was attacked in her home by someone she knew. A man who'd been a neighbor for 15 years and a frequent golfing buddy of her husband showed up on her doorstep intoxicated. He wanted to come in and said he was there to meet her husband, Tim, for a drink. Rosemary didn't know that her neighbor had already called her husband and knew he wasn't home.

She thought it was a bad idea to let her neighbor in so late because only she and her young son were at home, so Rosemary decided to call her husband, Tim, who was out of town. When she turned to pick up the phone, the neighbor shoved her, wrapped something around her neck, and pulled it tight.

She fought him and got a hand under the ligature. As she was asphyxiated, Rosemary asked him, "Why me?"

Her attacker looked at her without emotion and said, "I don't know."

He was a strong man in his forties, and Rosemary stumbled and fell face down in her kitchen. Her neighbor got on her back and started pulling the ligature tighter. She tried but couldn't manage a scream to alert her son, who was just upstairs. With her free hand, she reached out and pulled over a kitchen table chair. The chair was made of heavy metal and made a loud bang as it hit the glass tabletop and, finally, the floor. The sound was enough to alert Rosemary's 12-year-old son Jason, who came running down the stairs.

Jason saw his mother on the ground with a man on top of her. The man was trying to strangle her with what looked like a necktie. His mom was kicking her legs and trying to scream, but no sound was coming out, and then she stopped and went limp. Jason ran to the kitchen drawer, got a knife, and ran over to stab the man attacking his mom. He managed to stab the man once, but the knife handle broke before he could try again. Unsure what to do now to help his mother, Jason shoved and hit the man until he fell off balance. The neighbor, startled by Jason's attack, got up and ran out the door.

Rosemary was barely conscious, but she was able to get a few breaths of air and started to stand when the neighbor ran back in the open door and punched her in the forehead and the mouth. They struggled, but Rosemary was able to stand up this time, and she ran for the door. She and Jason ran across the yard to a neighbor's house.

The man got up to follow them with the necktie still in his hand, but he stumbled and fell in the doorway, ripping the necktie in half. He decided to run for his car instead.

JOHN CAREY

It wasn't long before Rosemary's neighbor, 48-year-old John Carey, was arrested.

Police collected evidence from the scene of the attempted murder. They collected part of the necktie that was left behind and photographed the ligature marks left on Rosemary's neck.

Part of the investigation included the seizure of John Carey's computer. Police found hundreds of images depicting strangulation along with a 90-second "snuff film" in which a man strangles a naked woman seemingly to death. John Carey had 978 unique searches on his computer containing the search term "asphyxia."

CHARGES AND TRIAL

Carey was charged with attempted murder, battery, home invasion, and assault. During the trial, his defense team claimed that he and the victim were having a consensual sexual encounter and that strangulation was part of their sex play. Carey took the stand to confirm this story.

Prosecutor Kim Faitella told another story for the jurors. She explained that John Carey was attempting to bring to life his sexual fantasy of strangling a woman to death —the very thing the images on his computer depicted.

The jury didn't believe Carey's defense. They were swayed by the hundreds of strangulation photos and other media presented in court by the prosecution. They found John Carey guilty of all charges.

The media outlets covering the trial called Carey the "Hamilton Strangler."

Before sentencing, Rosemary Diskin made a statement to the court.

"John Carey has shown no remorse at all, and his fabricated stories are disgusting and sick.

I would not be alive today if it weren't for Jason. John Carey did not stop strangling me after my son appeared in the kitchen, so what do you think he was planning to do after he murdered me? John Carey was going to strangle me to death, and it's a horrible, horrible feeling to think of what he would have done after that.

John Carey is an evil, horrible, dangerous, twisted man who robbed my entire family of their sense of security.

I had the dreadful fear that when people saw me, they would think that I had some relationship with him or shared his sick perversions. It was horrifying what John Carey did to me, and I don't think I'll ever completely recover or understand why he chose me."

Rosemary said almost one year after the attack, her son is still terrified and locks himself in his room if he is home alone. She said she suffers from nightmares, has PTSD, and still has neck pain. She said the attack had affected her husband, mother, and sisters, who all have trouble sleeping because of what happened.

John Carey didn't change his plea of not guilty but made a surprising statement in court.

> "I did wrong...There's nothing I can say to Rosemary and Jason that's going to make them feel any better. I can only apologize to them...I was walking in the dark for many years. I walk in the light now."

Carey ended the statement by saying he abused the trust of the neighbors he'd known for 15 years and now prays for the family.

Carey was sentenced to 20 years in prison and five years of parole.

In 2010, John Carey attempted to overturn his conviction. He was unsuccessful.

Thanks to her son, Jason, and how hard Rosemary Diskin fought to stay alive, she would be instrumental in helping police solve a decades-old Massachusetts cold case in 2022.

~

21 YEARS EARLIER

On the afternoon of June 30th in Beverly, Massachusetts, three public works crew members stumbled upon a young woman's body. She was dressed in a tank top and shorts, and her body had been brutally beaten.

She was found 25 yards from the northbound lanes of Route 128. The young woman was identified as 20-year-old Claire Gravel. She was a computer science major at Salem State College who had completed her sophomore year.

After collecting evidence from the scene, investigators retraced Claire's final movements. The night before she was found, she had been at Major Magleashe's pub, a twenty-minute drive from where her body was found. She'd spent the evening with her friends and fellow soft-ball team members. Between 1:30 am and 1:45 am, she was reportedly dropped off by a male friend at a credit union next door to her apartment in Salem.

The pub owner told police there was nothing unusual about Claire or the friend group. He said he wasn't aware of any issues the group had while at the bar.

Other bar patrons gave a different story. There were claims that a man was bothering Claire at the bar, and the man drove a white truck. Police investigated this but came up with nothing.

Claire's friends were questioned and said she was fine when she left the pub. Her friend Cheryl Chamberlin claimed the male friend who dropped her off at the bank was someone they all trusted to get her home safely. He was the last of her friends to see her alive, and police ruled him out as a suspect.

Cheryl said, "I really don't want to believe that she was severely beaten. They [the police] emphasized how she was severely beaten. I couldn't go to sleep last night because every time I closed my eyes, all I could see was her body all strangled."

After an autopsy, the medical examiner determined Claire died from asphyxiation from strangulation. The police declined to say if she was sexually assaulted, and the newspapers criticized them for refusing to release any other details of the crime. They would only say that Claire was severely beaten. Months passed, and the police turned up no other leads or suspects.

CLAIRE GRAVEL

Claire Ann Gravel was born in Massachusetts in 1966 to Mary Louise Gravel and Robert J. Gravel Sr. She graduated from North Andover High School in 1983. While studying at Salem State College, she worked on a work-study program for Salem State's Department of External Affairs.

Claire was popular among her friends and coworkers. One of her coworkers described her as a "bright girl who was always smiling." She loved to play softball and made most of her friends through the game. She was described as a "regular" at Major Magleashe's pub with her group of friends.

Claire's mother, Mary, described her daughter to the media as a beautiful girl with freckles, red hair, and blue eyes. She told the local newspapers that police initially thought her daughter was jogging when she was attacked, but she believed her daughter was taken, murdered, and dragged to the area where her body was found near Route 128.

Claire's family buried her at Bridgewood Cemetery in North Andover after a funeral service at St. Michael's Church.

A CASE GONE COLD

Over the decades, dozens of witnesses and people of interest were interviewed, but police never had a suspect. In 2009, Detective Lieutenant Elaine Gill, who was leaving, handed over Claire's case file to another state trooper. She had been investigating Claire's murder for over 20 years and had kept a box containing the case notes under her desk the entire time.

Three years later, in 2012, investigators had a new lead, and though they wouldn't disclose it at the time, they would go on to say that evidence recovered from Claire's clothing would be instrumental in solving this case.

Despite the breakthrough in 2012, it would take another

decade for investigators to gather enough evidence to reveal the name of the man who they believed killed Claire Gravel: John Carey.

It was now 2022, and John Carey was due to be released from prison in less than a year. Rosemary Diskin, now 70, was worried about the implications of his release. She and her son Jason, now a grown man, were concerned that John Carey could still threaten their family and others.

To Rosemary's relief, in August 2022, a now 63-year-old John Carey was charged with the first-degree murder of Claire Gravel by an Essex County Grand Jury. The police had John Carey's DNA from the necktie he used to strangle Rosemary Diskin. They matched Carey's DNA to DNA found on Claire Gravel's tank top. John Carey would have been 27 years old at the time of Claire's death.

JUSTICE FOR CLAIRE'S FAMILY

Claire Gravel's mother passed away in 2015 without knowing who murdered her daughter. Claire is survived by her father, two brothers, and a sister. Her father, Robert, now 86, has been carrying around a photograph of his daughter in his wallet since her murder. He told reporters, "She [Claire] is always on my mind. When I leave here, on my way home, I'm going to the cemetery to go talk to her and tell her what happened."

Claire's brother, Bob Gravel Jr., said, "Today is the first day on the road to justice, the day we didn't think was coming but is finally here, and now we're just waiting for the court process to take its course."

MOVING TOWARD A NEW TRIAL

John Apruzzese, John Carey's lawyer, asked the judge for a motion to turn off the video monitor during his arraignment. He said he was concerned about tainting a potential jury pool for the new trial. The judge denied the request, noting that pictures of Carey were already recirculating in the media from his previous trial. An older Carey was shown on camera with white hair and black glasses.

On a Zoom video arraignment, the alleged murderer of Claire Gravel yelled the words "not guilty" into the microphone when asked for his answer to the charges that he murdered the Salem State Student in 1986. Carey now faces a new trial and a likely much longer prison term.

It will be interesting to see if the police can connect other strangulation deaths in the area to the Hamilton Strangler in the coming years.

Get the whole volume of stories here!

Killer Case Files Volume 5

GET A FREE BOOK, AND MORE . . .

1.DID YOU ENJOY RITUAL KILLERS?

The #1 thing you can do to help me is to leave a review. Reviews elevate visibility and help new readers find all my books. Please consider leaving a review. I would really appreciate it!

2. Don't forget to grab your free book!

As a thank you to my readers, I created a special volume of my other series *Killer Case Files: 20 All New True Crime Stories.* You can download it right now for FREE in e-book or audio format at this link. Go to JamieMalton.com for information.

3. Would you like to join my **Launch Team** and receive a free e-book volume before it's published?

If you are a reviewer on any of the well-known plat-forms like Amazon, Goodreads, or Instagram, you could receive an advance review copy of my future volumes. I'd love to have you on my official launch team!

Go to JamieMalton.com and sign up on my mailing list for more information.

4. To see all of my books - including multi-volume bundles and boxed sets - visit my Amazon author page here. My Author Page

Next up in Curated True Crime is Holiday Hell

Thank you for being a reader.

Sincerely,

Jamie Malton

ABOUT THE AUTHORS

Jamie Malton is an award-winning, American, non-fiction writer. She is the author of Killer Case Files: Jamie Malton's Best True Crime Series which is an anthology of crime stories where the author examines the homicides perpetrated by murderers and serial killers.

Drawn to the how and why of real crime stories and fascinated by the detailed police work, DNA reconstruction, and genetic genealogy, she started writing her books to share the details of these stories with her readers.

For book research, she splits her time between the USA and European destinations, where she often visits some of the places where crimes have occurred.

With criminal apprehension and victim restitution as a personal cause, she donates a portion of her book sales to charities that fund DNA reconstruction to solve cold cases and charities that support the families of murdered victims.
You can reach her at JamieMalton.com.

AIDEN GALWAY

Aiden Galway is an author with an insatiable curiosity for unraveling the mysteries of the human psyche. He's particularly interested in disappearances, unsolved crimes, peculiar histories, and unexplained mysteries.

Born and raised in County Donegal, Ireland, Aiden's passion for storytelling started at an early age. Aiden's goal as a true crime writer is to shed light on heinous acts and explore the motivations that drive individuals to commit them.

Printed in Great Britain
by Amazon